The 7-Slide Solution™

Telling Your Business Story in 7 Slides or Less

7-Slide Solution™

The 7-Slide Solution™

Telling Your Business Story in 7 Slides or Less

Paul J. Kelly

SILVERMINE PRESS

7-Slide Solution™

Library of Congress Cataloging-in-Publication Data

Kelly, Paul J.
    The 7-Slide Solution™

        Includes index and bibliographical references
        ISBN 1-4196-2003-7

Published by:
Silvermine Press
113A Kings Highway North, Westport, Connecticut 06880

ACKNOWLEDGMENTS

This book has been more than ten years in the making. It is the result of countless hours of thought, research, testing ideas, writing, facilitating seminars, revising, trying new ideas, revising again, feeling the excitement of some ideas working, and the disappointment of other ideas going down in flames.

I am particularly grateful to my clients who allowed me to devise and refine the business story process, and who were understanding when things didn't always go as smoothly as I would have liked. I also want to thank the hundreds of seminar participants who challenged me when my thinking was fuzzy, and who responded positively when I was on target. Not everyone has the privilege of testing his ideas with business professionals. The ideas in this book would be simply that – a collection of ideas – without them.

I want to thank Ellen Simmons, with whom I have collaborated for over 20 years. Her editorial suggestions and revisions often led to arguments, but were always on target. She helped make this a much better book.

I also want to thank Susan Spadaccini, whose attention to detail and standards of excellence kept me focused and produced a work of which I am quite proud.

David Essertier was invaluable in providing both editorial feedback, as well as the kind of visual insights that I lack.

Finally, I want to recognize the comments and contributions of the following people, each of whom represents years of experience in the corporate, non-profit, and educational fields of communications: Marcia Brown, Daniel Callahan, Roy Cohn, Mark G. Evans, Stan Juozaitis, Kevin McEvoy, Antonia Pennisi, Paul Ruane, and Nancy Thomas. Their advice and counsel helped give me the perspective I needed to complete the book.

CONTENTS

7-Slide Solution™

Introduction

A ccording to *Time Magazine*, approximately 30 million PowerPoint® presentations are conducted in the world each day. Whether those meetings are held in large corporations or in government offices, in law firms or in non-profit organizations, the purpose of these meetings is the same: to exchange information so that decisions can be made.

If you have ever been asked to deliver a critical presentation or proposal as part of a meeting, then you have probably faced a blank Microsoft® PowerPoint® presentation graphics program template and wondered, "How will I get my message across? How will I keep the audience interested while I make my case?"

A most likely problem is that you have facts and data that are important and must be shared – more facts and data than your audience is likely to comprehend or care about. You're faced with the dilemma every communicator has faced since language was invented: what do you leave in and what do you leave out? Often – too often – most presenters get the balance wrong.

WHY DO I SAY THIS?

Research indicates that more than 90% of people have daydreamed during meetings, and more than 70% have brought other work into the conference room so that they can catch up on what really matters to them. Nearly 40% of the people surveyed said that they have actually dozed off during a meeting.

The dilemma becomes particularly acute at meetings and communications that are directed at disparate groups – people who don't share the same jargon and enthusiasm that you and your colleagues do. I call this communicating at the "boundaries." Boundary communications take place in budget reviews, strategy sessions, sales calls, task force updates, board meetings, and hundreds of other formal and informal get-togethers between

Microsoft and PowerPoint® are either registered trademarks or trademarks of Microsoft Corporation in the United States and/or other countries.

functions. These communications are the essential links between your desk and the organization at large. These are often the most important communications in terms of gaining needed consensus and support for the big initiatives that drive your business.

With so much at stake, you face a challenge every time you prepare for meetings and presentations: how to balance your credibility and deliver the facts of your message while engaging your audience members in a presentation that they will remember – and want to act upon.

WHAT THIS BOOK IS ABOUT

This book is about building effective presentations. It examines work-related communications and what they say about you. This is about what you can do to communicate effectively with your colleagues and peers, your bosses, your bosses' bosses, customers, contractors, and all the other people who need to understand you so that you can get your job done. People who, frankly, may not always share your interest in a topic or proposal.

This is *not* a book about public speaking. This book does not provide advice about stance and gestures, timing and cadence. Nor is it about graphic design, or dramatic sound and lighting techniques.

This book is about how to re-think the *structure* of presentations. This book provides a platform for sharing information that is as old as civilization itself – *stories*. And this book will show you how to tell a compelling business story by *using 7 slides or less*.

Using stories as the basis for an effective business presentation works. I use it in my business. Leading Fortune 100 companies use it in theirs. That's because stories hold people's attention. Stories provide a context or frame of reference for the facts and information that must be communicated: it's easier to remember the gist of a complex story than a string of statistics. The techniques and step-by-step processes that you will learn about in this book have been applied by professionals around the world, in thousands of meetings and presentations.

Whatever your field, if part of what you do involves persuading other people, then this book will help you become an architect of successful presentations:

- How to plan them
- How to build them
- How to make them work

WHY DO YOU NEED THE 7-SLIDE SOLUTION™?

The **7-Slide Solution™** allows you to communicate everything you need to say in the least amount of time, with the fewest number of slides, with the greatest intellectual and emotional impact. The reality is that you'll be able to tell in 7 slides (or less) what some people can't tell in 50.

The **7-Slide Solution™** is a way to position yourself in your professional environment. Think of having a reputation as the person who gets to the nub of a problem and finishes meetings early. The **7-Slide Solution™** is a skill that will contribute to your career advancement, no matter what your field.

The **7-Slide Solution™** is a practical approach to building presentations that appeal to the way people actually think about information. It is a process for building your presentations using a structure that supports every idea ever conceived.

- It taps into our innate familiarity with stories – people just love a story, and will even sit through a bad one, if only to hear how it ends.
- It uses a structure that journalists, moviemakers, writers, and advertisers have mastered – but that has been missing in business presentations.
- In a noisy world, this process helps you rise above the clutter and capture your audience's attention.
- It is different from that which your audience is accustomed – different, but welcome.

HOW TO USE THIS BOOK

This book is organized into three parts.

Part I reviews the challenges of persuading other people. These chapters give you insights about how people receive and process information in a "data-rich" environment, and how difficult it is to persuade other people to accept your viewpoints using facts alone. As you read, you will discover that people are, generally speaking, pretty poor at processing facts. You will also learn what happens when people are overwhelmed with facts and information – not a good outcome.

Part II tells you how to plan and design the **7-Slide Solution™** for effective business presentations. As you go through these chapters, you will

Each chapter of this book includes "bonus information" that relates to the text, such as the thoughts and wisdom of prominent writers and theorists.

follow a step-by-step process for building a business story. Using a storyboard, you will be able to design a presentation that will deliver maximum impact. All in 7 slides or *less.*

Part III tells you how to actually build and construct the **7-Slide Solution™** – slide by slide. You will be able to use each slide to fill a distinct role and purpose in your presentation.

It isn't easy to stand out from the crowd in 30 million daily presentations. You may not be able to persuade every audience every time. However, if you take the time to follow the ideas in this book, then you will improve your success rate – and you will never look at business presentations the same way again.

Part I: Persuading Others In Data Rich Environments

Chapter 1
The Marketplace of Ideas

This is a book about communicating in today's workplace. An environment where facts and ideas are traded every day. A marketplace where the *internal* competition for attention and resources can be more intense than anything external competitors can offer. This book describes the principles that you can apply to win in the marketplace of ideas.

THE COMMUNICATIONS ENVIRONMENT

The structure of professional organizations has changed radically during the past twenty years, and every indication is that the evolution will continue. Whether you look at large, profit driven corporations or at non-profit agencies, the landscape is the same - "leaner" organizations that demand greater productivity from fewer employees.

As the management pyramid continues to flatten, tiers of middle management disappear and the chain of command throughout the organization is reduced. There are three consequences of this:

1. Senior managers have a wider span of control.
2. Junior managers have greater exposure to senior managers.
3. Both senior and junior levels must learn to communicate more effectively to outside resources – brokers, contractors, agencies, distributors, and other third parties that are increasingly called upon to fill the gaps created by these new "lean machines."

These developments, coupled with the explosion of data, create a dilemma that every large organization faces: aspiring managers eager to demonstrate mastery of their functions through exhaustive research and analysis are bumping up against decision makers with less time (or inclination) to listen to details.

The results can be devastating. Who hasn't heard the hated phrase, "Can you give us the 5-minute elevator conversation?" or "Give us the 30,000 foot view." Weeks of preparation down the drain.

Worse, this mismatch can cause a sense of organizational discord. The senior team can be perceived as out of touch, while the junior members run the risk of being branded geeks, or worse, not "strategic" (code for "a bit simple" in some organizations).

This is our marketplace, and we must be able to think, act, and communicate within its confines.

The technology that has flattened the hierarchy and reduced the chain of command has also had a real impact on how we communicate. The traditional business meeting is supplemented by forms of digital communications – webcasts, WebEx, "Chat Threads," and instant messaging – that add to the information load borne by overburdened managers.

Since many communication settings lack your physical presence, the ability to structure and develop presentations in a compelling way is more important than ever. If the communication is not sharp and to the point, then it will be ignored.

THE INFORMATION SUPPLY CHAIN

Every function within the organization gathers particular information in order to keep the wheels turning, improve performance, and move toward objectives. Every function must also produce communications for others to review, evaluate, and act upon.

This may be the most complex manufacturing and supply process in the world: the raw material (facts) is refined and processed into something that can be used by others. But rarely is one function's information fully understandable to another's function, so the "manufacturer" quickly loses control of how his or her "product" is used. What starts as a localized analysis can spread and be re-interpreted in dozens of ways throughout the organization.

All of this "manufacturing," "warehousing," and "delivery" of information makes for a very busy and noisy marketplace. Just as giant retailers attempt to bring in more shoppers by offering more merchandise, some people try to gain attention by offering more and more information. Also, just like retailers, if the "information inventory" isn't managed well, then the enterprise can become bloated, dysfunctional, and unprofitable.

THE COMPETITION FOR SHARE OF MIND

Wherever you work, you know that there is a real competition for resources – everyone is doing more with less. In order to get some of those scarce resources, the best possible case for support must be made. Due to management's increased span of control and workload, there is a risk that solid analysis can be lost in the rush to get things done. So, presenters often follow this logic:

- Management is focused on "higher order thinking," such as strategic issues and long-range planning.
- How can I break through and demonstrate *my* higher order of thinking to the boss?
- I'll demonstrate that I've studied the problem by organizing *all* of the facts and presenting a rock-solid position.
- I can use a series of bar charts, pie charts, bubble charts, and timelines to illustrate that I am a "strategic thinker."
- It may take 60 slides, but the boss will have no real choice other than to support my position.

Here are four reasons why that kind of logic is likely to backfire:

1. Who ever said that mastering all the facts was "strategic?" Al Gore mastered mountains of facts and couldn't win his home state when he ran for President.

2. A higher order of thinking often results from creative leaps that may have little evidence to support them. Einstein was not the most meticulous researcher, but few would argue with the height of his thinking.

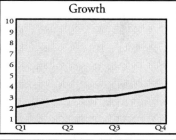

3. Graphics can just as easily misinform as inform. X and Y axes can be expanded or compressed. Pies can be divided in arbitrary ways.

4. Bosses do have a choice whether or not to support the proposal. They can (and probably will) shut down.

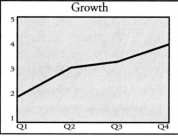

In the marketplace of ideas, more decisions are collaborative than ever before. Because managers' spans of control are greater, a broader consensus must be developed, often gaining support from the very functions against which you are competing for resources.

Think of your business environment as a stock exchange – and think of your ideas as an equity or stock offered on that exchange. The people who trade at the exchange have a finite amount of capital and resources to invest. Information provides the liquidity that the marketplace of ideas needs to run. Too little information, like too little capital in an exchange, limits the amount of trading that can take place. Too much information, like too much capital, creates an environment where trading can take place purely for the sake of trading.

The question every communicator in the marketplace of ideas must answer is, "How do I attract market participants and persuade them to buy my equity?" Bringing attention to new ideas becomes almost as important as the ideas themselves.

PRINCIPLES FOR WINNING IN THE MARKETPLACE OF IDEAS

Due to the demands on time and attention in lean business environments, there are some principles that you can apply whenever you participate in the marketplace of ideas.

Principles

- Be brief, but thorough
- Dazzle them with BS (Brilliant Stories)
- Facts are facts – and that's the problem
- Passion often wins out over logic
- The best attention from management may be to be left alone

- *Be brief, but thorough.* This is not a contradiction. The best communications are concise. Consider the Gettysburg Address – or even the TV listings in your local newspaper. A business presentation that fully covers the topic in the shortest period of time is the one that will be remembered – and acted upon.

- *Dazzle them with BS (Brilliant Stories).* Engaging your audience makes all the difference. This means simple graphics to tell the story, and a "hook" that will capture attention.

- *Facts are facts – and that's the problem.* Every function that competes in the marketplace of ideas is supported by facts, and everyone believes that his or her particular facts are the most important and compelling. People tend to think that the facts speak for themselves – that what seems perfectly clear to those who work with the data will be equally clear to everyone else. The truth is people can, and often will, misunderstand, misinterpret, and misuse facts because they view them from their own perspectives.

- *In the long run, passion often wins out over logic.* Find the ideas that make sense to you and that which you can take ownership. When you don't believe in your presentation, no one else will either. The net result will be damage to your credibility and reputation.
- *Ultimately, the best attention from management may be to be left alone.* When you present well-documented ideas in a concise and interesting manner, you provide a foundation for trust. This trust is often demonstrated by reducing control and increasing your independence.

Because business meetings are so important in the marketplace of ideas, it is worthwhile to consider what actually occurs during these sessions: What's going on inside people's heads as they process all of the information that is coming at them? How good are people at comprehending and processing what you are saying? What happens if they can't assimilate what is being said? Can real exchanges of ideas even take place?

Chapter 2
"Reading" the Minds of Your Audience

It is estimated that professionals in all fields attend approximately 62 meetings every month – that's an average of more than three meetings every working day. What are people thinking about during all of those sessions? How do they decide what is important and what is not important? At what point do they switch off? It would be great if you had the answers to those questions as you develop your presentations.

Since the 1950's, psychologists have been examining the various processes that most of us call just plain "thinking".. They consider how the mind takes in and manages information – in essence, the engineering behind the mind. All of this thinking about thinking is known as cognitive science.

In effect, insights from cognitive scientific research allow us to read the minds of other people because the research indicates how all of us handle the continuous flow of input, and tells us what happens when the flow becomes too great. This chapter reviews some of the ways we sort data and then presents tips on using these insights to design and construct "scientific" business presentations.

Cognitive Science

The field that studies the mechanics of human intelligence. Cognitive science also involves the investigation of the processes involved in producing intelligence in a given situation.

Collins Dictionary of Artificial Intelligence

SCANNING, LONG-TERM MEMORY, AND SHORT-TERM MEMORY

Perhaps the single most remarkable activity of the human brain is its scanning ability. Researchers have estimated that our brains can scan 350 megabytes of information per second, which is considerably faster than the best scanners on earth. We not only scan information from all of our senses, and do it all at once, but we instantly evaluate and assess the input and begin making decisions.

Brain Statistics

- People can scan about 350 megabytes per second. That's equal to over 1,000 of these books in one second.

- It is estimated that the lifetime memory capacity of the brain may be 280,000,000,000,000,000,000 (280 quintillion) bits.

- The mind stores information in thousands of "representations" that can be called on at will.

- Short-term memory, the "gatekeeper" of the mind that determines what to keep, is very slow. By one estimate, only 18 bits per second.

- For most people, 7 chunks of information is all they can hold in short-term memory.

When you walk into a crowded party, your mind takes in every face in the room, hears the background music and foreground chatter, senses whether it is warm or cold, assesses whether the lighting is bright or dim, picks up the aromas of the foods and perfumes, registers the general dimensions of the room and the decorations, and even determines who to speak with first. All of this occurs in less than a second – no scanner can do all this. You do it with virtually no conscious effort on your part.

That's why slides or other visuals are the foundations for business presentations – people grasp visual information much faster than spoken information. Your audience is always way ahead of you visually – they have read your message and have begun to interpret it and make some preliminary judgments before you even start to deliver your comments and explanations.

After the brain has scanned all of those billions of stimuli, what happens? Thankfully, a great majority of the input is lost forever. Just consider what would happen if you remembered everything you saw and experienced. You'd be so bogged down in trivia you would literally not be able to think.

Cognitive scientists have not been able to determine the extent of the average capacity of long-term memory. It seems incalculable. Most adults can remember events from their childhoods with real clarity; certainly our minds hold information about significant events and re-play them over and over. John von Neumann, a mathematician and computer pioneer (he invented the "bit"), has estimated that the lifetime capacity of the brain may be 280 quintillion bits. In comparison, an 80-gigabyte hard drive (basically, a top-of-the-line desktop computer) holds only about 690 billion bits.

Short-term memory is the "gatekeeper" between the scanning function and long-term memory. We cannot possibly send all of the information we receive into long-term memory. So our short-term memory capacity is used to determine what to reject and what to keep.

Cognitive science research indicates that our short-term memory works at an inverse rate to our scanning ability. Our scanning ability is *fast* – but our short-term memory is *slow*, by one estimate operating at approximately 18 bits per second at optimal levels. In addition, short-term memory has a very limited capacity, and it can quickly become overloaded.

WHEN THE GOING GETS ROUGH (INFORMATION-WISE), WE TUNE OUT

Professor Orin E. Klapp has identified six events that can occur when people become overloaded with information. The first is that we simply omit pieces of data. We fail to deal with all of the input.

A second occurrence is that the input becomes jumbled and we end up by processing erroneous information. For example, if I attend a party where most of the women are wearing black, I may "remember" that Jane was wearing black when, in fact, her gown was blue. I was so overloaded by the amount of data that I was scanning that I simply processed the wrong information about Jane.

Another problem that may occur is "queuing" the information in short-term memory with the purpose to "think about it later." The problem is that "later" rarely comes. New input crowds out the old and it becomes lost forever.

6 Bad Things That Happen When People Are Overloaded

1. Omitting information
2. Processing erroneous information
3. Queuing data for future consideration (which never seems to come)
4. Selective exposure
5. Discriminating with less precision
6. Escaping

As short-term memory becomes more and more crowded, people begin a process called "selective exposure." They rely on filters to screen out everything *except* a few selected inputs. For example, a listener at a four-hour environmental conference may tune out everything she hears that is not related to issues of bio-diversity. When bio-diversity is discussed, her mind focuses on it. When the third speaker in a row addresses other topics, she puts up her filters again.

Information overload causes all of us to take short cuts in sorting and storing inputs. This is why "eye witness" identification at a crime scene is considered so fallible. In the confusion and panic of the moment, a witness may "remember" that the perpetrator was short and fat with bristly blond hair, when in fact the villain was tall and thin and bald.

Finally, when overwhelmed with information, the brain may happily escape into a daydream or some other easier thought process. Too much data can seem like a flood, and we simply switch off.

SEVEN CHUNKS AT A TIME

Of course, the brain does not make errors or shut down all of the time – data does get through and our short-term memory capacity manages the inflow. Professor George A. Miller of Princeton University, a pioneer in cognitive science, reported as long ago as 1956 that the average person can hold and process only seven pieces of information in short-term memory at any one time. Researchers following Miller's work have recognized that the mind has the ability to "chunk" information – to instantly sort and group data so that it is retained as one fact or chunk. For example, a Social Security Number is composed of nine digits - because we must all learn our SSNs, we can recall all nine digits as a single chunk of information. However, whenever we give that information to another person, that individual has to write the number down as nine separate digits.

What happens when most people have to process more than seven chunks? They not only lose the extra chunks, they lose the entire message.

THE FILING SYSTEM OF THE MIND

Our brains are not hard drives: they are much more elegant and sophisticated. Where a computer breaks a file into bits (essentially 0's and 1's), our brains store information as "representations," or mental images, what most of us would call "ideas." That is, the mind takes in information and processes it into a representation that can be used again and again. Some of the representations can include:

- *Experiences.* From infancy on, the brain evaluates new information and stimuli against accrued experience. The older we get, the greater the database. If I closed my hand in the car door when I was five years old, that painful experience will stay with me and I will hold the representation as an event I don't want to repeat. My experience will also lead to representations of protecting my own children from similar accidents.

- *Concepts.* These include beliefs and values, such as "honesty is good and dishonesty is bad." These representations generally relate to intangibles – something learned rather than experienced directly.
- *Habits.* Like experiences, our habits are a convenient mechanism for representing a lot of the information that surrounds us. If it is my habit to only listen to views that reflect my own views, I will never be exposed to opposing views.
- *Fears.* Some information is represented as a fear or anxiety. If I represent the stock market as "dangerously risky," it's then unlikely that I'll give information from a broker much credence.

The False Consensus Effect

One finding of the cognitive sciences is the tendency to estimate how widely beliefs are held by others based on our own beliefs. Here's how it works:

- We evaluate other views and beliefs based on our own views and beliefs.
- We assume that the opinions of people who are attractive or powerful are similar to our opinions.
- We expose ourselves only to information that reinforces our beliefs.

There are thousands of other representations that humans hold in long-term memory – and because no two people are alike, their representations won't be alike, either. What is true for all of us is that we do process facts and data into ideas and representations – we do not store data. Our brains are not built that way.

As the adult mind evaluates new sensations and information against the representations of long-term memory, one of two things will happen:

1. The new data will be consistent with current representations and will be accepted (the "no-brainer").
2. The new input will be inconsistent with current representations and will be challenged, and challenge can lead to resistance.

When there is resistance, persuasion becomes necessary.

A SNAPSHOT OF THOUGHTS IN ACTION

To tie all of this information about cognitive science and "mind processing" together, consider this scenario...

A middle-aged man is sitting alone in an airport departure area, waiting for his flight to board. He is tired after a day-long presentation and is looking forward to getting home. More than anything else, he is bored. He looks over the shoulder of the traveler sitting beside him and *scans* the headlines of the newspaper she is holding.

In a matter of seconds, he is able to scan the entire page. He finds himself growing impatient because the woman is reading some articles (processing the information through the gatekeeper of her short-term memory) and doesn't turn the page quickly enough to satisfy his desire to scan. Then he notices a headline that says: "Men Over 45 Need Regular PSA Tests for Prostate Cancer".

His thoughts slow down as he decides whether or not to consider that information more completely. Based on some of his representations of experience and theories, his brain decides that the answer is "yes." The information is held in short-term memory as the man's thought process continues.

The man compares the data in the headline against the representations in his long-term memory. "I am over 45, and although tests like this are pretty painless, I don't like doctors. I really don't want to hear any bad news, but I have an obligation to my family to stay healthy. At any rate, my insurance will cover the cost."

The man makes a decision to call his doctor's office for an appointment next week.

A similar dynamic occurs among the audience members of business presentations. Each person has unique representations about the topic, and they will compare what is said or shown against their own representations. At some point, each person will decide to pursue the new information further – or to stop thinking about it.

"SCIENTIFIC" BUSINESS PRESENTATIONS

Use Cognitive Science to Improve Your Presentations

1. Recognize the limits of short-term memory
2. Anticipate how people will evaluate your message
3. Prepare for resistance

The good news from cognitive science research is that you can use these insights to become a better presenter.

The first step is to recognize the limitations of human short-term memory – do not try to deliver any more than seven distinct chunks of information at one time.

When short-term memory is faced with more information than it can handle, a bottleneck is created, and two phenomena occur. One is selective exposure: the mind works to hear only what it wants to hear.

The second result of a bottleneck is to over-simplify the information or to develop a bias. In this case, we "massage" or bend the information to conform to a simple solution.

The big message for all of us who must communicate information to others is that too much information is worse than boring – it actually inhibits the ability to make decisions by reducing the scope of issues people are willing to consider.

Finally, every presenter should prepare for – and welcome – some resistance. That's right, resistance is good. It means you've challenged some accepted ideas.

The advances in cognitive science can help you connect, engage, and influence your audiences' thinking. Bear in mind that although people have amazing abilities to scan and sort information, it is difficult to move from short-term memory into the core of memory that can be recalled and acted upon.

For that reason, weigh your data. Are there so many facts that people cannot possibly chunk it? If so, then cut it down.

Effective presentations work because they *influence* how people think. The cognitive scientists have interesting ideas on that topic as well.

Chapter 3
People Think In Ideas, Not Facts

Applying the findings that cognitive scientists have published means that "mind reading" is not as far-fetched as it seems. However, having some insights as to how the human mind works doesn't mean that we can *change* how the mind works.

This chapter discusses how presenters can *influence* how people think, and reviews some proven techniques for bringing influence to bear. Although there are some limits to just how much influence and persuasion any presenter can exert, a compelling case for your idea can be delivered. As professionals, we all like to think that we make decisions based on logic, but there is often a more potent component at work in the process.

According to the Newspaper Association of America, more than $245 billion was spent to change people's minds through advertising in 2004. Yet, in most mature product and service categories such as autos, consumer non-durable goods (like food and household products), and financial services, there are rarely dramatic shifts in market share as a direct result of advertising dollars spent.

Aside from those triggered by cataclysmic events, mind change is usually a slow process. It is a process that is so complex and individual that attempts to model it across the human species have not succeeded.

If the multi-billion dollar advertising industry is only minimally successful at changing minds, and the best cognitive scientists can do is to make cursory observations about it, what makes you think you can change minds in a single business presentation?

The reality is, you can't.

What you *can* do is influence how people think about a topic. That influence may encourage some audience members to begin the process of change within their own minds.

INFLUENCE, NOT CHANGE

5 Ways to Think Straighter

1. Recognize that people prefer distinct solutions – even if they are wrong – to shades of gray. Be forceful, even if it causes some level of controversy.

2. Be equally impressed with what has happened as with what has failed to happen (faith healers never "cure" visible diseases like acne – only "invisible" diseases like arthritis).

3. Don't draw conclusions from what happened under present conditions without considering what might have happened under alternative conditions.

4. Recognize that people don't usually optimize decisions (seek the best alternative), but establish an "aspiration level" – perfection is not necessary or, generally, appreciated.

5. Question information that is consistent with what you already believe as stringently as you would information that is inconsistent with your beliefs.

Most of us think that we have pretty good ideas - that our opinions and beliefs are sound and that, in fact, the world would be a better place if more people thought the way we do. Our ideas are bound up in the way we think of ourselves. They are the result of our upbringing and experiences, education, and values. In many ways, we *are* our ideas. It's human nature to be protective of our ideas, and to defend them against outside threats.

How easy is it to change our own ideas or beliefs? To start over again with a truly fresh viewpoint or theory? To give up a bad habit? Or try a new way of doing things? Even if we know an idea is outdated and possibly dangerous, we will often struggle to find a way to justify it before giving it up.

If it is so difficult to change our own minds, try to imagine how hard it is to change some one else's ideas or opinions or beliefs.

The truth is: ***No one ever changed anybody's mind but their own.***

The human mind is open to new sensations and ideas - as long as those new inputs conform in some way to what is already in the mind. In 1967, Rheingold Brewery introduced the first light beer – Gablinger's Diet Beer (notice the word "diet"). It was a dismal failure. Most beer drinkers at the time thought of a beer as a fun product or an indulgence. The last thing they wanted to think about was how many calories it contained. Five years later, Miller Lite was launched. The pitch? It's less filling – you can drink more. The

Gablinger's message didn't conform to beer drinkers' representations of what a beer should be. The Miller message, on the other hand, was worth considering. Did Miller change peoples' minds about the caloric content of beer? No. Did they influence people to think differently about what a beer could be? Absolutely. That influence resulted in a multi-billion dollar business.

INFLUENCE TOOLS

People can change their minds. Whether it's something mundane like changing beers, or something epic like race relations, actual and substantive change in attitudes, preferences, and beliefs does occur. But what can an "outsider" do to influence the way people think about things inside their heads? Here are four primary tools that a presenter can use to influence how people think:

1. *Logic.* This is rational argument – an approach that involves identifying and weighing factors, making an objective assessment, and then making a decision. When you use logic in your presentation, you demonstrate a systematic chain of reasoning that should make sense to everyone who sees it. Logic is most effective with peer groups who understand underlying research and are conditioned to look at issues from the same perspective as the presenter. Scientists, economists, corporate lawyers, and bureaucrats use logic among themselves. They are often lost, however, when they try to use the same approach with "civilians," because what is logic to an expert can be perceived as insider jargon to the uninitiated.

2. *History* or current events. Outside influences can shake up our cozy world of ideas. Stock market crashes, terrorist attacks, and company lay-offs can influence how we think. This approach involves identifying relevant examples, collecting data, and verifying or casting doubt on a particular idea. It often involves historical reflection and statistical proofs – the data that support the argument. Current events can influence if they are truly dramatic – or made dramatic by the presenter.

3. *Rewards.* These are the financial, physical, or emotional benefits of accepting a change from the status quo. Behavioral scientists (as opposed to cognitive scientists) believe that all behavior is governed by reward and consequences (Pavlov's dogs). People certainly like rewards, but don't always act in their own best interest.

4. *Re-Illustration.* This is the use of new words or graphics to present an existing idea. Einstein re-illustrated thinking about time by imagining what he could see if he were riding on a beam of light.

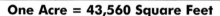

An example of re-illustration

One Acre = 43,560 Square Feet

As a fact, that isn't very memorable. If it can be re-illustrated, then it may mean more.

One acre is approximately the size of a football field without the end zones.

LIMITS OF PERSUASION

Think about the major mind changes that you have experienced in your lifetime. Did those changes come about *solely* because of any one of these tools? Do you always follow logical arguments? Do you make decisions only on the belief that "history repeats itself?" Do you always do the things that provide the most reward? If you are shown a new way to look at a problem, does that guarantee that you will change the way you think about the problem?

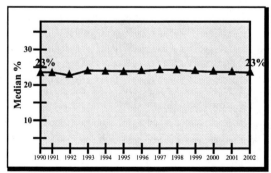

Current US Smokers

Source: *US Centers for Disease Control*

Of course not. These tools are limited. Here are some examples:

Logic would dictate that people must recognize that smoking is dangerous to health. Yet, billions of dollars in public service ads, extensive educational programs in schools, dire warnings on packages, and general societal hostility have failed to persuade many people who smoke. In fact, over a 12-year period, smoking incidence has remained steady at about 23% of the U.S. population.

History shows that American men, women, and children have gained weight during the past 20 years to the extent that obesity is now a major health threat in the United States. The historical research shows that obese people are more likely to suffer from diabetes, coronary disease, and high cholesterol levels. Further research indicates that obese people also suffer from depression and are less productive in the work force because they lose more days at work. Despite this historical data, most Americans have not changed their eating habits.

US Historical Weight Trend 1963 - 2002

Male	Female	10 Yr. Old Boy	10 Yr. Old Girl
1963 - 166.3 lbs.	1963 - 140.2 lbs.	1963 74.2 lbs.	1963 - 77.4 lbs.
2002 - 191 lbs.	2002 - 164.3 lbs.	2002 - 85 lbs.	2002 - 88 lbs.

Source: US Centers for Disease Control

The *rewards* of completing a high school education provide much greater earnings and career opportunities than do the prospects for dropouts: dropouts will earn $200,000 less than high school graduates in their lives. Despite improvements, the high school dropout rate remains at approximately 11% of the student population.

High School Dropout Rates of 16 to 24 Year Olds

1980	1985	1990	1995	1996	1997	1998	1999	2000
14.1	12.6	12.1	12.0	11.1	11.0	11.8	11.2	10.9

Source: US Census Bureau

While these influence tools are powerful, they are not enough to motivate a mind change. To do that, the influence tool must be made *personal*. Each individual must see how the message applies to him or her. Advertisers, politicians, lawyers – *everyone* struggles with the challenge to make a message compelling.

MAKE A COMPELLING CASE

> **Com-pel-ling** *adj.* 1. To drive or urge forcefully or irresistibly 2. To cause to occur by overwhelming pressure
>
> *Dictionary.com*

You can build a compelling case for your position by using the right combination of logic, reward, and history. Also by adding re-illustration to clearly convey what you mean, but that's not enough. You need to stir in some emotion as well.

People start smoking because they think it's "cool." Can they define cool? Probably not. Does it matter? Not at all. Trying to persuade a smoker that it is not cool has a higher chance of success than citing disease statistics or life expectancy charts.

Some people eat too much because they enjoy food. Other people overeat because they are lonely or feel incomplete in some way. Explaining to people that being overweight will cause them more loneliness and less enjoyment may have a stronger impact than historical waistline trends.

Most experts agree that kids drop out of school due to low self-esteem. These students believe that they can't compete. Showing a kid who thinks he's a loser a chart that depicts his lifetime income as tens of thousands less than his "winner" classmates does more to reinforce negative self-image than to combat it.

Using emotion to influence the way people think makes some presenters uncomfortable. Professionals like to pride themselves on being objective, steely-eyed rationalists. But emotion flows throughout every enterprise: competition (threat), strategy (hope), control (fear), profit (survival), image (relationship), and morale (motivation).

The question is: how can you infuse enough emotion into a presentation without losing the objectivity that most organizations favor (or demand)?

> **Res-o-nance** *n.* Richness or significance, especially in evoking an association or strong emotion.
>
> *Dictionary.com*

RESONANCE: THE MYSTERIOUS PERSUADER

For a presentation to be compelling, it must "resonate" with the audience. We've all experienced resonance at some point. Perhaps it was a politician whose words stirred you to such an extent that consideration of his or her opponents became superfluous. Or, that special person who made dating others a waste of time.

When words or images resonate, they tell us that something is so very right or very wrong that other messages fade away. For most Americans and many others, the phrase, "We hold these truths to be self-evident, that all men are created equal" is so perfectly phrased that there is no need to add to it.

These words and images resonate with us – either positively or negatively – because of the principles or values that we associate with them and the emotions they evoke. They resonate for us because we can form stories about them in our minds. These stories conform to and reinforce the representations we have in our minds. They just feel right.

Can we explain why certain words or images have such a powerful impact? Not very well. That's why resonance is so mysterious and hard to achieve. One thing is sure, facts by themselves do not resonate. The total number of deaths at the World Trade Center disaster was 2,749 – a horrific number. But the number is not the story – the story is of courageous firefighters and the despair of families. That's because most statistics don't create a response if they cannot be linked to something stronger and more emotionally impactful.

Resonance is hard to come by. Advertisers, "spin doctors," and other communications experts fail more often

Avoid Emotion at Your Own Risk

"...the selective reduction of emotion is at least as prejudicial for rationality as excessive emotion...emotion probably assists reasoning, especially when it comes to personal and social matters involving risk and conflict".

Antonio R. Damasio
The Feeling of What Happens:
Body and Emotion in the
Making of Consciousness

Antonio R. Damasio, Chief of Neurology at The University of Iowa, has worked extensively with patients who have suffered damage to the areas of their brains that process emotions. One of his findings is that while such patients are quite capable of analyzing facts and follow similar thought processes as the rest of us in solving problems, they find it very difficult to make decisions. Dr. Damasio believes that this is so because these patients are no longer able to process the knowledge and thoughts that we call emotions. In essence, they lack the gut reaction.

Favoring so-called objective, fact-based presentations may be neither objective nor fact-based when it comes to cognitive science.

than they succeed. No one ever influenced anyone to think about making difficult decisions without appealing to the emotional as well as the intellectual side of human nature.

PEOPLE THINK IN IDEAS, NOT FACTS

We can use facts and logic, we can evoke emotions, and we can build resonance – and we still struggle to persuade others to consider our position. Research has shown time and again that people cannot always relate to facts and cannot easily process facts without some means of connecting facts to experience. In short, people think in ideas, not facts.

Ideas provide a frame of reference for facts. A statistic like "market share" is understood by most professionals because they have an idea of what a market or geography is. The statistic is a handy data-gathering tool – but it only works if someone already has an image in mind.

Are Statistics Facts?

Is gross domestic product (GDP) a fact? Does it reflect the actual state of the economy?

The answer is NO. GDP is a statistic that can be calculated in a number of ways. We have an idea that GDP represents total goods and services produced, but we don't know all of the data that was used to derive the final figure.

J. Steven Landefeld, director of Bureau of Economic Analysis, was quoted in the *New York Times* as saying, "Our job is to get the *general* snapshot of the economy *about* right." [Italics mine] Not very factual, is it?

Ideas come before our understanding of facts. An acre equals 43,560 square feet, or approximately the size of a football field minus the end zones. That makes sense to a person from the United States, where land is measured in acres and where football is a national passion. But the same information would be meaningless in India, where land is measured in hectares and cricket is the national game.

If people are so good at processing ideas and forming them into representations, then why are they so often poor at communicating ideas?

The written word can't do it alone. Much of the world's population was, and remains, illiterate. Yet complex ideas like religion, myth, ethics, and cultural norms are understood by billions of people.

Visuals do not always help. Although a picture can tell 1,000 words, an image is often open to interpretation. What's art to one person is trash to another.

Recitations of facts and numbers do not help. Many people are what the author John Allen Paulos terms "innumerate" – ignorant and fearful of numbers.

Words, images, and numbers are only tools of communication. It's how those tools are used that matters. It's about how communication is structured that makes it effective or not.

SO HOW DO WE COMMUNICATE IDEAS?

The structure people use to communicate ideas to one another – the structure that has been used to communicate ideas since before civilization – is *stories*. When you design and build business presentations as stories, people will understand your ideas and will be persuaded to consider a change.

Successful communicators set reasonable goals. They know that they may be able to *influence* other people to consider new course, but they recognize that they will not be able to *change* anyone's mind. In presenting the most compelling case for their proposals, they provide powerful "food for thought," using ideas to frame the facts and emotion to create resonance for those ideas. When all of these elements are combined in a story, then real communication occurs.

Chapter 4
Stories: A Powerful Platform

It's a fact – cognitive scientists and the researchers who study the activities of the human mind have determined that we are all idea processors. That is, the human brain is hard-wired to think in ideas, not facts. Ideas support the facts, and give us a context for using information. Long before cognitive science became an academic discipline, in fact, before there were any academic disciplines at all, mankind had learned that the best way to communicate ideas and facts was through stories.

This chapter takes a closer look at stories and how they work – and how stories can work for you as the foundation for communicating ideas.

THE REALLY BIG IDEAS AND HOW THEY GOT SO BIG

Think about some of the truly significant ideas that are part of any civilization – ideas like religion, culture, political systems, or economics. Ideas which humans have developed and spread and upheld throughout the centuries. Did you ever wonder how these complex notions began and how they came to be accepted by millions of people?

Of course, there have always been scholars who dedicated their lives to the promulgation of grand ideas – but they have usually been relegated to monasteries and universities. They would publish their theses, but just like today, few people took the time to read them. In fact, until the middle of the 20th century, the vast majority of the world's population was illiterate (over a billion still are), so they were unable to read the opinions and considerations of the masters.

Sophisticated ideas came to unsophisticated people through stories, parables, and legends. Stories that were transmitted by apostles and itinerant peddlers, by great explorers and common sailors.

These became the ideas that were passed from generation to generation, the stories that were repeated and ritualized in the schools and religious houses. These stories may use some facts – but mostly, these stories resonate because they speak in a unique way.

Stories never stop. Stock markets make dramatic moves based on stories that spread from trading desk to media outlet to investors. Religions expand through the stories of evangelists. Politicians gain or lose power based on the stories they project.

STORIES ARE THE MOST POWERFUL COMMUNICATION DEVICE EVER CONCEIVED

Has This Ever Happened To You?

A doting parent is reading a favorite story to a very young and sleepy child. And as the little one begins to doze off, the parent realizes how tired she is after a long day. So she decides to skip just a few pages of the story to speed the whole household toward slumber.

What happens?

The sleepy child immediately awakens knowing that something has gone very wrong!

The structure of stories is so universal that all of us can follow it instinctively, and instantly recognize when the structure has been altered. Is it possible that we are "hard wired" to follow a storyline?

We like to think of ours as the most advanced era of communication in history. With broadband connections, WI-FI, mobile technologies, and satellite, we are connected wherever we go. But these are just communication enablers. Have you ever thought about what is being transmitted through these tools? Mostly, stories.

The media – print, TV, film, music, and much of the Internet – is fueled almost exclusively by stories. Without stories, there would be no entertainment industry, or news industry, or public relations.

Governments have always used stories about heroic leaders and the struggling populace who will gain through politicians' programs.

Advertisers thrive on stories. Ads showing housewives saved by a cleaning product, testimonials from satisfied vacuum cleaner users, families brought closer by telecommunications. Stories are how things are sold. Marketers try to weave their brands into the story of your life – "you simply cannot live without this…"

Successes in commercial enterprises are told as stories that become legends. You may have heard the story of Sam Walton flying over rural America in his small plane looking for "green field" sites – those locations near smaller towns that could easily accommodate the acreage required for a Wal-Mart. Or the one about Amazon.com founder Jeff Bezos giving up a lucrative financial career to sell books over the fledgling Internet.

We are literally swimming in stories. They surround us. They define our lives, our cultures, our organizations, our hopes and our disappointments. We love them. So why is a good story so hard to find in the conference room?

One reason may be that large organizations are risk-averse. There seems to be a sense of comfort and efficiency in knowing that everyone is communicating the same way – even if they are not actually saying much. The reliance on best practices becomes a substitute for creative thinking.

Another reason may be that organizations feel better about themselves if they do things differently from the outside world. The bigger and more powerful the organization, the more bizarre the protocols can become. Religions, bureaucracies, governing bodies and the like have collections of rituals, acronyms, job titles, and traditions designed, it seems, to utterly confound the outside world.

Can you think of any other part of your life where you communicate in as stilted and artificial a way as you do at work? Can you imagine asking someone out on a date by providing an agenda and objectives? Or review your family vacation plans by starting with situation analysis? Can you picture demanding that your kids provide a risk/reward ratio to make a case for using the family car? If it's silly in real life, why is it accepted in business life?

A "NEW" COMMUNICATIONS PLATFORM

One task of management is to create "platforms" on which work can be carried out. Political parties have platforms to guide their candidates. IT departments have platforms like SAP to ensure different software programs work together. Human Resource functions provide a salary platform to ensure that no one is overpaid or underpaid.

In the same way, many presenters, from all fields and disciplines, have come to rely on a standard platform for organizing the scheme or flow for a business presentation. It looks something like this:

- Agenda and objectives
- Background (lots of statistics)
- Body of the presentation ("what I'm here to talk about")

- Conclusion
- Recommendations

What's wrong with this platform? It is a tried-and-true formula that has worked for generations. Well, here are some thoughts on that.

Basically, this scheme is tolerable because we are so conditioned to it that we can follow it without thinking. But this is a vehicle for relating facts. The statistics, not the ideas, become the "stars." The audience is relegated to observer status. Unless the statistics are startling, there is little in this scheme to engage the audience.

In particular, although an agenda and objectives are essential to any meeting, there is no need to state them *during* the presentation. Whenever possible, describe the agenda and objectives *before* the meeting. That way, the audience knows what to expect and why when the meeting opens.

The "what I'm here to talk about" portion of the presentation should be the most compelling. Unfortunately, these critical passages are often an onslaught of statistics. If the group is still following along, this may be the point where it tunes out.

The conclusion should be the "eureka moment" in the presentation – the culmination of what the presenter worked so hard to convey. Disappointingly, this can be the moment when the audience sighs, "Eureka – it's over." That's because people drew their own conclusions much earlier in the presentation.

Recommendations are something of an anti-climax – if the case was made, the audience should be making the recommendations.

This standard presentation structure of "Agenda through Recommendations" has become obsolete. It has become a detriment to effective communication because it has been repeated so often it lacks the ability to engage. Communications structures come and go. For decades the dramatic structure of a Lowell Thomas newsreel was the way news was delivered. Now it seems corny and overdone. Silent movies featured dramatic close-ups meant to convey emotions. They seem positively goofy now. It's time to re-think the standard business presentation structure.

Organizations can create a new communications platform by insisting that every important business presentation be a story that is told to the audience.

You do not have to be creative or especially clever to do this. All you need to understand is that every good story that was ever told was built the same exact way.

Part II: Designing the 7-Slide Solution™

Chapter 5
Every Good Story Has the Exact Same Structure

Cognitive science recognizes that the human mind is a processor of ideas. People communicate ideas through stories. But not all stories are as clear or convincing as others.

This chapter examines how good storytellers follow a specific structure and maintain a desire to see what happens next and how you can apply those storytelling techniques to design a **7-Slide Solution**™ for your business presentations.

We are surrounded by stories – dozens and dozens of them every day.

Early in the morning, the clock radio sounds off with news stories, weather stories, and sports stories...

Early morning television offers a range of serious and frivolous stories over coffee...

The morning newspaper is a compendium of stories from around the country and around the world...

At the office, colleagues tell stories about how they spent the weekend or about the miseries of their commutes...

"Down time" during the workday can be used to surf the Net, which provides more stories...

At the dinner table, each family member recounts the day as stories...

Watching TV or a movie in the evening is another way to take in some stories…

And reading a book or magazine before drifting off to sleep means some more stories…

At times, we even dream in stories…

THE STRUCTURE OF STORIES

Stories are universal and an integral part of our lives – but how are good stories put together so that we can always understand them? Lots of people have wondered why stories are so effective – dramatists and scriptwriters, poets and novelists, journalists and historians, and professors from all fields of academia.

For thousands of years, good stories have been – and continue to be – so effective because they use the same basic structure. It's easy to conclude that something so standardized might be predictable – but even though we instinctively recognize the structure, we can't wait to see how it will play out.

HOW DO GOOD STORYTELLERS DO IT? - START WITH A PREMISE

Expert storytellers begin with a premise – the point they wish to make with the story. Sometimes called the theme or central idea, the premise directs the entire story. The premise is the message.

For a good example of a story premise, check the TV and movie listings in your local paper. These concise descriptions can summarize a two-hour movie in a line or two. If you had to describe a favorite film to a friend, what would you say? Chances are you would tell that friend the premise.

Most stories never state the premise, but the way the story is built clearly delivers the message. The success of the story is measured by the fact that the audience "gets it" without being explicitly told.

One Premise - At Least Six Stories

Good stories seem to last forever, even when we have heard and understood the premise many times before. Here are just some of the ways expert storytellers have used the premise, There's no place like home, over the centuries…

- *The Odyssey*
- *Gulliver's Travels*
- *Hansel & Gretel*
- *The Wizard of Oz*
- *ET: The Extra-Terrestrial*
- *Finding Nemo*

The premise is the point when good storytellers first think about resonance - the emotional as well as intellectual impact of the story that will connect with people and make them remember the message.

Good storytellers know that a story cannot have more than one premise. There is only one message to a story: having more than one premise makes a story unwieldy and, ultimately, meaningless. This is a discipline that business presenters should follow whenever they prepare a meeting.

EMBRACE CONFLICT

When the premise has been identified, good storytellers take it apart to isolate a core conflict. This is the "hook" that grabs and holds the audience's attention.

The 5 Building Blocks of *Every* Successful Story Ever Told

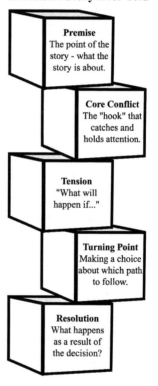

If Romeo and Juliet had received the blessings of both their families and embarked on a long and happy marriage, there would not be much of a story, and we probably wouldn't even know their names. It is the animosity and discord between the two families, and the sad fate of the lovers, that creates our interest.

All good stories – tragedies and comedies alike – are built around an inherent conflict. The *Star Wars* films use the core conflict of good vs. evil; *Jurassic Park* is based on the core conflict of man's inventions vs. nature's order.

Why is conflict so interesting? Because people are naturally curious and want to see what happens whenever two forces or ideas are in opposition to each other. Perhaps it says something about us as a species, but we love conflict – especially when we are able to observe it from afar.

BUILD TENSION

Once they have isolated a core conflict, storytellers examine it, expand it, think of consequences, and build *tension*. Tension means that the core conflict is reviewed in several dimensions. Tension is built through examination of implications or consequences.

The storyteller then answers his or her own questions: good things will happen if certain actions occur, or bad things will happen if other events take place. Tension in a story takes the audience on a ride and, when done well, continues to build on the desire to see what happens next.

OFFER A CHOICE

When the core conflict has been examined and tension is at its highest, the good storyteller offers a choice. The fork in the road. The moment of truth. The climax or turning point. A decision must be made and we sit on the edge of our seats waiting to see if it will be the right one.

PROVIDE RESOLUTION

The turning point leads to the *resolution* of the story – the result of the choice. This can be the "happily ever after" scene in a story like *Sleepless in Seattle*, or a lifetime of regret in a story like *Citizen Kane*.

The resolution accomplishes a number of things. Most importantly, it *resolves* the core conflict. Resolution shows the results of the choices made. It also ties up the loose ends. It leaves us feeling satisfied.

THE DESIRE TO SEE "WHAT HAPPENS NEXT..."

Storytellers use the structure – premise, core conflict, tension, turning point, resolution – in a series of scenes. Each scene builds on the previous and transitions to the next. When done well, it creates a desire in the audience to see what happens next. This desire gives the story momentum and energy. People are engaged. They are not leaving until it is over.

Have you ever attended a business meeting where you couldn't wait to see what happens next? Where you absolutely had to see what was on the next slide? Where the presenter kept you on the edge of your seat?

Why is the desire to see what happens next so rare in business meetings? Everyone has a distinct and natural interest in doing what's right for the organization. At a business meeting, there is a shared level of interest. Why not exploit that interest? It should be easy to create a desire to see what happens next when the audience shares the same interests.

Some people might say that the very interest of the business audience is the problem: the audience members are so familiar with the issues that they've heard it all before. That's what is so intriguing about the story structure. Despite seeing hundreds of detective stories, there is always an audience for crime movies. Most love stories are alike (boy meets girl, boy loses girl, boy wins girl back), but there is an endless demand for more love stories. The story structure engages people, even when they have heard similar stories before, because they are curious about the storyteller's perspective. The truth is, *how* a story is told is at least as interesting as *what* is being told.

I believe that the same curiosity extends to business presentations.

THE STORY OF THE 7-SLIDE SOLUTION™

This book is built on storyline. Here it is: my premise is that e*very professional presentation can have the impact of a good story and can be told in 7 slides or less.*

What's the conflict? It's the dilemma of providing enough data to be credible vs. streamlining communication so people can understand and make decisions.

Where's the tension? 30 million presentations a day! Jack Phillips of the Chelsea, Alabama-based ROI Institute figures that $60 billion of productivity is lost in the U.S. each year due to poorly planned and executed meetings. As data expands, the need to organize and communicate effectively becomes urgent.

So choose. Do you want to continue to use the tired Agenda-through-Recommendations platform for your presentations? Or are you willing to consider a structure that will make you stand out from the crowd and influence people to see things your way?

The resolution? Adopt the story structure as your presentation platform – let the structure that even young children recognize work for you.

DESIGNING THE 7-SLIDE SOLUTION™

It is possible to use the methods of expert storytellers to meet the needs of a business presentation. It is if you keep some simple guidelines in mind:

1. *Think of every slide as a scene.* Each slide is important to the dynamic of the storyline. Just like a story, each slide can build on the previous one and provide a transition to the next one. Slides should not be wasted with superfluous information or "nice to know" insights.

2. *Develop a premise, and then prove it.* Each storyline should have a single, provable premise. The premise is not stated overtly in the story, but it drives every scene.

3. *Conflict is interesting, facts usually aren't.* Most presenters want to avoid conflict because they feel it will upset the audience and lead to arguments. Nothing is further from the truth. People love conflict and want to see how it will be resolved.

4. *Stories are only satisfying when conflicts are resolved.* When you describe conflicts in a professional situation, you must be ready to resolve them.

This seems simple enough – so why don't more people use it? Probably because they don't know where to start.

Chapter 6
Storyboarding The Presentation

While every presenter has his or her own way of preparing, one very effective way is to "storyboard" the presentation before opening the computer and launching PowerPoint®.

In this chapter, the concept of a storyboard and its use will be described. This chapter introduces the practice of using each slide in a presentation the way a director uses a scene in a movie – to communicate a complete idea. Then, this chapter provides some specific tips on using a storyboard and how to make storyboarding your routine.

WHAT IS A STORYBOARD?

If you are in a marketing or communications role, you are probably familiar with storyboards. The Disney Animation Studios invented the storyboard in the 1930's. Webb Smith, a Disney writer and "storyman," is generally credited with the brainstorm. The method is still very much in use today: everything from 30-second commercials to full-length feature films, and even large-scale business meetings, are planned, visualized, and choreographed using storyboards.

Storyboard *n.* A panel or series of panels on which a set of sketches is arranged depicting consecutively the important changes of scene and action in a series of shots (as for a film, television show, or commercial).
Merriam Webster's Dictionary

You don't have to be an animation artist, or even especially creative, to get value from a storyboard. You can plan and build a more compelling business presentation by stealing the best ideas from the best minds of the creative community.

"DISPLAYED THINKING"

Many people plan a presentation by going straight to PowerPoint®. They think, "Slide #1 will be the title, slide #2 the agenda, then some background data, then..." That's a little like a movie director taking a script and hiring actors and crew, then wandering around town looking for locations that support the story line. It's inefficient and random.

Other presenters develop detailed outlines of what they want to say. Word processing programs provide templates that structure an outline at a touch of the tab key. The structure of any outline is hierarchical: major headings are supported by sub-heads that are further supported by "bulleted" points, facts, and insights. While I favor being prepared, detailed outlines can, because of the hierarchical structure, diminish creativity. The presenter can become so trapped in supporting all of the minor points (II, A, 1, b, [iii]) that dramatic flow is lost. The final presentation becomes a visual translation of the outline – stilted and mechanical.

People don't think in a structured, hierarchical way. People represent information in various ways and test what they hear or see against experience. That's why storyboarding is so valuable. Sometimes referred to as "displayed thinking," a storyboard conveys a visual line of reasoning. It not only shows what ideas should be included in the presentation, but also how each idea relates to other ideas to form a dramatic flow. A storyboard also allows the presenter to see what facts should or should not be included in the presentation. Finally, a storyboard allows the presenter to sketch out the 7 slides (or less) that will become the actual presentation.

MAKING A SCENE

Like a story, a professional presentation communicates a sequence of events to demonstrate a change. Storytellers call these events "scenes." A film may have 40-60 story events or scenes. A novel may have even more. The good news is that most business presentations require only five to seven scenes. Why so few? Because your audience is living the same plot as you are. There is less need to explain what's going on and more opportunity to get right into the "action."

How to Develop a Successful Scene

1. Plant a question
2. Evoke a specific emotion
3. Answer the question
4. Move the story forward

You can construct a successful scene by following a few simple guidelines.

A scene is not a story in itself – but it does have a beginning and an end. The beginning should plant a question that will engage the audience. A question can be planted in a number of ways – challenges, simple truths, or claims. If you think of your favorite adventure film, each scene sets up a situation and you, as an audience member, asks, "Uh oh, how will he or she get out of this?"

Each scene should evoke a specific emotion in the members of the audience. This is how resonance is built into the story. In the action film, the emotion is usually anxiety or fear.

The question planted at the beginning of the scene should be answered – or at least partially answered. When the hero somehow out forces the villain, the question is answered.

The end of the scene should move the story forward. Each scene of the story should maintain the momentum and keep the audience's desire to see what happens next.

Here is an example of how the opening scene of a presentation about a productivity problem could be structured:

> "How have productivity levels changed in the last year? (*Question*). Growth has been impressive, but we are still below industry levels (*emotion – need to measure up*). Although productivity increased by 30% (question answered), here's what I intend to do to improve to industry standard levels (*move the story forward*)."

A scene like this resonates better with the audience than a simple "data-dump" for a number of reasons:

1. People don't like unanswered questions. They become engaged because they want to see how the presenter will answer the question.
2. It taps into emotions. Every scene should stir the emotions a bit. When all the scenes are linked together, they should stir them a lot.
3. Once the question is answered, there is a sense of relief and also an increase in credibility for the presenter.

CHOOSING A PERSPECTIVE

Sometimes called "point of view" or "POV" in storytelling, perspective has a major impact on how a story is received. Stories can be very personal ("I/we") or more distant and objective ("it"/impersonal "they"). For example, "*We* (personal) have increased productivity 30% in the last year." Or, "*Research* (objective) indicates that the industry norm is 92%."

There are some general rules to follow when deciding which perspective to use.

Not Hard & Fast Rules for Choosing Perspective

1. Specify emotions to evoke
2. Don't mix perspectives
3. Use personal perspective for good news
4. Use distant perspective for bad news
5. Use personal perspective when the presenter is fully credible
6. Use distant perspective when the facts are compelling

First, think about the emotions you want to evoke in the audience. If you want the group to feel closely involved, consider the personal perspective. For example, to get the audience's competitive juices flowing, you could say, "*We* are falling behind *our* competition in three key areas..." However, if you want to encourage the group to approach the subject more intellectually, you could say, "Recent reports show a performance gap versus the competition..."

Don't mix the perspectives. Avoid starting out with a personal approach such as, "We are excited about the results," and then switch to a distant perspective like, "but *studies* show a 3% failure rate..." It undermines the credibility of the presenter to appear to take credit for successes while side-stepping the responsibility for failures or disappointments.

The personal perspective (I/we) is appropriate for good news ("As a team, *we* topped *our* goals for the fifth straight year!") or when the presenter has a great deal of personal credibility ("In *my* 20 years in the business, *I* have never seen such cutthroat competition...").

The distant or objective perspective is often used for delivering bad news ("Records indicate that the trend is downward") and when the research itself is so compelling that it can speak for itself ("The latest government figures show a decrease...").

In subtle and obvious ways, perspective affects the way an audience experiences you and your presentation. You must decide if you have or want to project enough personal credibility to use the I/we perspective. It's a critical design decision – do you want the audience to relate to *you* or to the data? It's up to you to decide if the research is compelling enough to tell the story or if it needs some personal enhancements from you. There is a discipline that good presenters follow, and a consistent perspective is one element of that discipline.

HOW TO "BOARD" YOUR IDEAS

Once you have determined a perspective, you are ready to build the storyboard. You may have seen storyboards that are very sophisticated with high-end illustrations and lots of color – but this level of sophistication is not necessary for planning an effective business presentation.

Take a large sheet of paper (legal size, if available), and lay it out horizontally. Across the top third of the page, draw the following...

The Presentation Storyboard

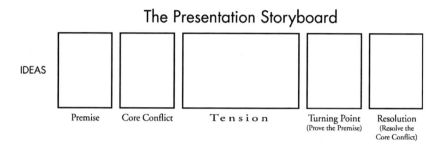

IDEAS

Premise   Core Conflict   T e n s i o n   Turning Point   Resolution
(Prove the Premise)   (Resolve the Core Conflict)

This is where you will design the platform of the story using the five key elements – premise, core conflict, tension, turning point and resolution.

Then, in the middle of the page, draw a large rectangle and title it "Facts/Evidence."

FACTS/
EVIDENCE

This is where you will note what facts are needed to support your story.

Finally, across the bottom third of the page, draw seven rectangles. These correspond to the scenes of your story and will serve as the base for the seven slides (or less) that will become the presentation.

A workable storyboard looks like this...

The Presentation Storyboard

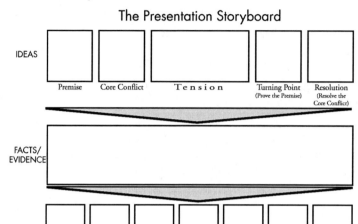

With this tool, you can see the entire story laid out on a single sheet of paper.

In the following chapters, you'll see how to use the storyboard, to build the scenes that will engage your audience by creating the desire to "see what happens next..."

MAKE STORYBOARDING YOUR ROUTINE

Storyboarding is valuable because it allows you to plot the key ideas of your presentation in sequence. It also allows you to see exactly what facts are needed to support the message – what to bring in and what to leave out.

The format of the storyboard lets you build each scene of the story. Every scene should plant a question for the audience to consider, evoke an emotion in order to create resonance, and then answer the question and move the story forward to the next scene.

As you develop the story, you will want to determine a point of view – generally, either a personal or more distant perspective. At that stage, you are ready to take paper and pencil to "board" the story.

You may be saying to yourself, "This seems like a lot of work – is it worth it?" Well, I've found two things to be true when I use storyboards...

1. It's easier each time I do it.

2. It makes for a better presentation each and every time.

If you want to build the kind of presentations that persuade people to think differently – really differently – about your proposals, you should consider making a storyboard part of your routine.

Chapter 7
What's Your Premise?

Stories are the most effective means of communication that mankind has ever used – or ever will use. That's because all good stories follow the same structure.

Good stories resonate with the people who hear them: resonance is what brings the story to life.

Where does resonance begin? For successful storytellers – and business presenters – it starts at the beginning. Before digging into the research, before creating a single slide, resonance begins with the development of the *premise.*

This chapter examines what a premise is and its role in the story. The chapter takes a look at the power and emotions that every audience brings into a meeting and offers some specific techniques for developing the premise for your business stories.

WHAT IS A PREMISE?

When a friend tells you, "I saw a great movie last night," you probably respond, "What's it about?"

What are you really asking?

Of course, you're hoping to get some sort of plot summary. If your friend says, "Well, the movie opens with a long tracking shot over Manhattan, and then zooms in to a corner of Central Park," you know that however good the movie may be, your friend's version is going to be awful. However, if she says something like "It's the story of man overcoming inner demons to find love" you might be more interested. Or she might say, "It's like *Star Wars,* only funnier" – a summary that works because you have a mental representation of the famous sci-fi film.

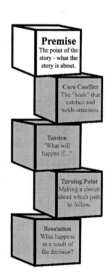

Premise
The point of the story - what the story is about.

Core Conflict
The "hook" that catches and holds attention.

Tension
"What will happen if..."

Turning Point
Making a choice about which path to follow.

Resolution
What happens as a result of the decision?

At the same time, you're hoping to get some sense of the emotional impact. If your friend tells you to "bring a box of tissues when you go to this movie", or "I laughed so hard my sides hurt," you'll get a sense of the emotional impact.

Those two elements – the plot summary and the emotional impact or resonance – are how *premises* of stories are built. The premise is a statement of what the story is about and what it does for the listener.

Because the human brain seems to be engineered to respond to stories, all of us have the ability to quickly summarize a story – to "encapsulate" the main points and to make judgments based on the capsule, not the entire effort. Most people can re-tell a good story in a concise way so that others can grab onto it – because the *premise* is clear. A badly told original story equals a badly told capsule – the story can't be transferred to other people and just fades away.

Good presentations are the same. If you think about the best presentations you have seen, you can encapsulate the main points. That's because the presenter had a strong premise and that premise came through to you as an audience member.

The premise is the "take away" of the story or presentation – what the presentation is about. The premise is also known as:

- The Hypothesis, if you want to be academic
- The Moral of the Story, if you want to be spiritual
- The Central Idea, if you want to be practical
- The Gist, if you want to get down to basics

WHO IS THE AUDIENCE?

Earlier, you saw how the premise, *There's no place like home*, is told by various writers and filmmakers. Let's face it, even though the premises are the same, the *Odyssey* is a lot different than *Finding Nemo*. That's because the stories are meant for different audiences.

In order to make a compelling premise, you must know who the audience is.

People attend business meetings for different reasons and with different points of view. Some people are there because they are sincerely interested in what's being said. Others are there because they want an update on what's going on. Some are there because they were told to attend. And some people are there because they want to appear interested in the subject even if they are not.

While each business audience is different, there are three dynamics that you can assume will come into play whenever a group of people attends a presentation:

1. *Power.* People take on different power roles depending on the structure of the group.
2. *Persuasion preference.* People find certain persuasion techniques (such as logic or reward) more motivating than others.
3. *Emotions.* People bring their emotions with them, but rarely display them in professional settings.

When possible, you can profile your audience in terms of these three dynamics to understand what they currently do, think, and feel.

THE POWER PROFILE

Broadly speaking, of the people who can influence a decision, there are two kinds of power:

1. The Power to say "Yes" – usually held by one or two people.
2. The Power to say "No" – held by everyone else.

The power to say "yes" is typically held by whoever controls the purse strings on a particular issue. Usually, that is the highest-ranking person in the audience, but not always.

The power to say "no" is held by a broad range of people. Relatively low-level people can exercise veto power by refusing to go along with higher-up decisions.

The power to say "no" extends to outside functions. Technical experts from accounting to warehousing can scuttle a proposal by invoking their expertise. It's hard to argue with experts, and these "no" votes carry weight.

Where and How Power Exists

Organizational: Based on position within an organization. Directors have more than managers, VPs more than Directors, etc. Recognition of status often (though not always) resonates with these people.

Technical: Held by people with a real or perceived expertise in a particular area such as IT, law, or finance. Technical research and testimonials often resonate with these people.

Tactical: Held by people on the front line. Sales and operations are examples of typical tactical influence positions. Issues like workload, morale, recognition, and generally making their lives easier resonate with these people.

Can your presentation satisfy every need for every power base in your audience? Probably not. Can you still create a story that resonates? Maybe. Here are some tips for creating resonance for diverse powers and influence:

1. *Focus on the common good.* Don't attempt to satisfy every need. Construct your presentation to demonstrate how broader constituencies (multiple functions) will benefit.

2. *Make allies.* You don't have to do all the persuading yourself. Develop champions within the group and let them persuade others. This is best done before the meeting, but you can build allies by directing your conversation to those who have the most to gain.

3. *Take serious disagreements "off-line."* Once again, this is best done before the meeting. If disagreement erupts during the presentation, see if you can address it later so that it doesn't poison the rest of the group.

Acknowledging a power need is only one contributor to an effective business story.

THE PERSUASION PROFILE

4 Persuasion Tools

1. *Logic:* Rational argumentation to demonstrate a systematic chain of reasoning that makes sense to everyone who sees it.

2. *History or Current Events:* Identifying relevant cases and verifying or casting doubt on a particular idea.

3. *Rewards:* The financial, physical, or emotional benefits of changing the status quo.

4. *Re-Illustration:* Using new words or graphics to present an existing idea, such as death tax vs. estate tax.

Remember that **no one ever changed anybody's mind but their own.** You must try to determine what will influence the audience to accept your idea.

Will they respond best to a logically sequenced line of thought or will they be more influenced by historical and current events? Will financial or other rewards sway them or should you re-illustrate the issue so that they can see it differently?

While people are not locked into any one persuasion method, they will often demonstrate preferences. Group dynamics can change what is and is not persuasive. If one audience member appreciates structured logic but three others only want to see what is in it for the company, then reward may trump the one person's preference for logic.

Here are some ideas for creating resonance with different persuasion preferences:

1. *Don't try to persuade everybody.* You can drive yourself to distraction trying to include a "pinch of history" with a "dash of logic," topped with a "splash of re-illustration" in order to please everyone in the audience. Few stories of any kind appeal to everyone. There's no reason to believe yours will either.
2. *Mix persuasion tools – but not too much.* Your story can have a dominant persuasion approach (for example, logic) but also draw on history, offer rewards, and re-illustrate certain points. Make sure to use the tools to make the story clearer, not just to satisfy one audience member's preferences.
3. *Go with your strongest hand.* If you determine that one persuasion tool is the strongest for a particular story – go with it. You can instill enough passion and credibility into the tools you choose to overcome any preferences of individual audience members.

THE EMOTIONAL PROFILE

People are emotional creatures. They want to satisfy both their rational and irrational sides. In fact, cognitive scientists believe that emotion is essential to decision making.

Emotions are not static - they change with the situation. Whenever possible, you should try to evaluate the typical emotional climate of the group – while recognizing that it may change minutes before or even during the meeting itself.

Most people experience possible loss more intensely than potential gain. As an example, psychologists and cognitive scientists have made studies of gamblers. They note that gamblers will protect a sure gain but will take risks to avoid probable losses. For that reason, it is often more persuasive to "go negative" than it is to accentuate positives.

By "going negative," I mean frame your story around potential loss, since loss is usually felt more dramatically than gain.

HOW TO DEVELOP A COMPELLING PREMISE

Knowing your audience is critical in designing and constructing your business story and in formulating your premise. When you are able to decide what the audience is most likely to do, think, and feel about your idea before the presentation, you can then determine how you want the audience to react during and *after* the presentation.

How to Develop a Premise

1. Select the best idea to communicate.
2. Frame the premise.
3. Consider emotions.
4. Choose one and only one premise.
5. Write the premise as a complete sentence.

A Case Study:
The 7-Slide Solution™ in Action

For the remainder of this book, the following situation will be used to design and build a 7-Slide Solution™:

Customer Service Department facts: Total staff = 350 people in 3 regional call centers; Total department budget = $30 million.

The current situation in the department is as follows:

- Significant budget cuts were introduced last April.
- Since then, call wait times have increased every month.
- Employee morale is low.
- Customer complaints are high and increasing.
- Several important service contracts are up for renewal.

So far, management has tried the following solutions: supervisor re-assignments; software upgrades; specialized training; efficiency bonuses; shift re-scheduling; temporary hirings

The manager has some ideas about how to resolve the situation and is developing a strategy presentation for a cross-functional group of senior managers.

From that point, there are five simple and related steps that go into the development of a compelling premise – the "what the presentation is about" capsule that people can recall and explain to other people.

Select the best idea to communicate. This is the single idea that will have the greatest resonance for your audience. Boil that idea down to its absolute essence. Remove all qualifiers like "estimated," "preliminary," and "subject to" (these terms weaken a premise and make it less interesting). Reduce or eliminate all adjectives and other unnecessary words. Don't think about potential audience reactions (that will come later) – just get the premise clear in your own mind.

The premise of your business presentation must be easy to comprehend. When you present your idea for change in a conference room, you are the expert. That's both good and bad. It's good because you know what you are talking about. It's bad because most experts forget what it's like not to know.

Frame the premise. As politicians demonstrate every day, how an issue is framed influences how people think about it. A good example of framing is the drive to repeal inheritance taxes in the U.S. Long called an "estate tax," the issue was dead with most taxpayers, who thought of estates as something rich people had. It didn't resonate. But call it a "death tax" and people become angry. The first frame results in disinterest: "The government wants to tax rich people. So what?" The other produces outrage: "They even want to tax you when you're dead."

To frame a story, list of all the possible ways people could think about the issue you are presenting. There are usually *dozens* of frames for any issue.

FRAMING THE STORY PREMISE

For example, I could frame the Customer Service department story around image: "Our reputation in the industry is being compromised." Or, I could approach the story, and my audience, from the position of morale and motivation: "People are stressed and likely to leave…"

The framing of the story is the place where you make the overt effort to meet the power, persuasion, and emotional needs of the audience.

When you select a frame, you are playing to the audience. This is the time in the design process that you are most sensitive to the specific power and emotional profiles of the listeners – the remainder of the story (conflict, tension, and resolution) is what you believe to be most important.

"Framing is about getting language that fits your worldview. It is not just the language. The ideas are primary - and the language carries those ideas, evokes those ideas."

George Lakoff
University of California

Consider the emotions that you want to evoke. Think about the feelings that you want to resonate in your audience members as a result of your presentation.

Just as there are many ways to frame a story, there are several emotions to tap:

- Pride
- Desire for gain
- Peace of mind
- Peer pressure - keeping up with the competition
- Fear of loss

To name a few…

The "Tell Me More" Test

To test the strength of your premise, answer these questions:

- Is the idea phrased in a way that people have seldom heard before?
- Is the idea likely to create the desire to see what happens next?
- Is the idea clear so that people can grasp it without explicitly telling them what it means?
- Does the idea have an emotional as well as intellectual impact?
- After the presentation, will the majority of the audience be able to summarize it in one sentence?

Choose one and only one premise. When you have framed the story and decided on the emotions you want to engender, a few powerful premises may be revealed. But – you must choose the right premise.

The right premise will be of interest to those who share your views – and it will attract the interest of those who don't.

Why is it so important to use only one premise for each story? People really can't concentrate on more than one story at a time. Try to imagine a movie about young lovers overcoming their families' hatred while simultaneously battling the forces of nature – "Romeo & Juliet Visit Jurassic Park" – which story would you focus on?

Although each story can only have one premise or message, a meeting or presentation may have more than one story. In these cases, you must complete the first story before beginning the second one so that the audience can encapsulate each story separately.

Write the premise as one complete sentence. Complete sentences are what we use to communicate complete thoughts. If you cannot express your premise in one complete sentence, then it's a sure bet that no one else will be able to, either.

More than one sentence will cloud the premise. In fact, if you require more than one sentence, you probably have more than one premise.

If your premise can be expressed as something less than one sentence – some sort of fragment - that may indicate some fuzziness in your thinking. This could be the start of an unfocused and rambling presentation.

GO TO THE STORYBOARD

With all of this information about the audience, and guidelines for developing a compelling premise, it's time to use the storyboard to begin to design the presentation about the Customer Service problem.

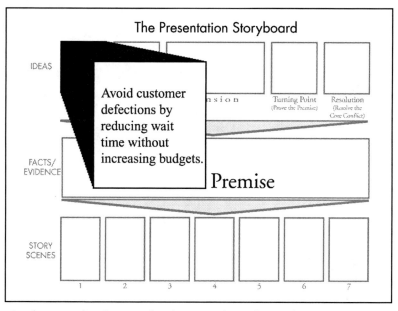

In this case the decision has been made to frame the story around sustainability: current operations must be sustained and improved within the framework of a tight budget that cannot be increased. Customers and competitors are becoming aware of the fact that service levels are deteriorating. The emotions that will be evoked are the flip side of sustainability – loss.

This story is about maintaining the current status in the market by stabilizing a dangerous situation. The story is not about growth, or improving productivity, or boosting employee morale.

If the presenter is wrong and the premise doesn't resonate with the audience, then he or she loses. To me, that's a better option than trying to make the story about sustainability, and growth, *and* boosting morale.

The premise – what the story is about – carries the entire story from beginning to end. The premise is what creates resonance with the audience and allows people to encapsulate the story so that others can understand it. In many stories, the premise is never stated directly – in the movie *ET: The Extraterrestrial,* you never heard the words, *there's no place like home* – but that's what the movie is about.

In order to develop a compelling premise, it is certainly helpful to know the audience and to understand the power, persuasion, and emotional profiles that are likely to come into play during the presentation. Because that is not always possible – and even when it is – the first step in developing the premise must be to select the single best idea to communicate.

However, one of the most difficult decisions any storyteller or presenter makes is to choose *one* premise and cut off all the other possibilities. That decision, though, is the difference between a compelling story and haphazard collection of ideas.

From there, the premise should be framed to meet the needs of the audience, and should incorporate the emotions that the presenter wants to evoke. Finally, the premise should always be expressed as a complete sentence so that it is clear to everyone – including the person developing the presentation.

Chapter 8
Conflict: The "Hook" That Every Presenter Looks For

Every good story has the same structure: a premise, core conflict, tension, turning point, and resolution. What engages an audience is conflict. People simply *love* conflict.

In this chapter, *conflict* is described not as a fight or obstacle between two opposing parties, but as the natural tension that attracts attention to a story. Because stories are as old as humanity, conflict is universal in the stories we tell – so why isn't it a part of a business presentation?

This chapter recommends that conflict be the organizing scheme of effective business communications, and provides the techniques for using that scheme.

In Search of "Hooks"

Frankly, I've never been comfortable with the word "hook" as it applies to grabbing the interest of an audience. I've never been sure what it means – is the audience a fish or a group of potential addicts? It doesn't seem to be a particularly apt metaphor for the most important element of any communication between humans – gaining and holding people's attention.

Nonetheless, hook is a term that resonates with most presenters.

Advertisers are in constant search of hooks. Whether it is musical, visual, verbal, olfactory, or subliminal, to create advertising means striving to break through the

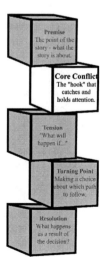

clutter and grab some attention (by one estimate, American consumers are exposed to more than 1,300 advertising messages per day). So there's quite a bit of clutter to break through.

Musicians use the term to describe a catchy "lick" or riff that will leave listeners humming their tune all day.

Storytellers search for a good hook as well. Movie trailers are a prime example of a hook. So are the jacket summaries and the first few lines of a novel.

Business presenters also seek to find appropriate hooks. How many times have you chuckled politely at some executive's stammering attempt at humor, or cringed at a lame skit meant to loosen up the audience, or shielded your eyes from some over-designed visual animating its way across a screen?

Of course, if you are even an occasional presenter, it's hard to be too critical because before long it will be your turn to stare at a blank PowerPoint® template and ask yourself, "What's *my* hook?"

The Human Condition

Let's face it: as a species, humans are not a happy lot. In history, if we are not fighting animals for a few scraps of food, we are fighting nations over wealth and territory. If we are not struggling to make a living, we are agonizing over ways to find happiness. We are never satisfied. Once one set of needs (like survival) are met, we begin the struggle for the next set (like comfort).

Our working lives reflect this condition. Imagine the CEO who tells Wall Street, "We're pretty happy with the ways things are – we're not going to change a thing." We are all struggling: to get things done, to get the resources we need, to be recognized and promoted.

The news media understands this aspect of the human condition. There is nothing juicier to a journalist than two powerful political forces with opposing viewpoints.

The entertainment industry exploits this unique frailty. What would *People* magazine be without high-profile divorce stories?

The sports establishment understands this. Sure, there's the conflict of the games themselves – but the side stories are always more interesting to the fans: the aging superstar against the upstart rookie or the troubled journeyman fighting his demons after leaving rehab. It's the stories we remember, not the scores.

Your organization is rife with conflicts. The battle against the competition is the obvious one – but that's the tip of the iceberg. Growth vs. cost containment, employee morale vs. stockholder satisfaction, productivity vs. employee quality of life – modern organizations are hives of conflict.

A general dissatisfaction with the status quo is what keeps the wheels of humanity turning. It's not so much that we like conflict. It's that we understand it so thoroughly from our own lives. More importantly, we can relate to struggles as if they were our own.

We are irresistibly *drawn* to conflict because we think there may be something to be learned from how a conflict is resolved.

> Happy families are all alike; every unhappy family is unhappy in its own way.
>
> *Leo Tolstoy*
> *Anna Karenina*

Picture this scene:

In an airport, you notice a man and woman talking intensely with each other. It's clear that there is some disagreement. The man is gesturing energetically and the woman looks like she's about to cry.

You move a little closer and overhear the following:

Man: "It's a fabulous opportunity. A huge increase in pay and a chance to gain some real exposure in the home office."

Woman: "All of our friends are here, and we've lived here for years. Besides, it's so expensive out there. I love our house here. We didn't see a single house there that even comes close."

Man: "It's my career. A chance to move forward. This could lead to really big things."

Woman: "The kids are so happy here. I hate to uproot them."

Man: "If I turn it down, we can pretty much kiss off my getting another offer any time soon."

Woman: "It's all about *you*..."

Man: "No, it's not. It's about *us*. We'll have more income. You'll be happy there, and the kids will like it, too. I guarantee it."

What you've witnessed is a *conflict*: two people with different goals trying to resolve an issue.

- If you've never had such a conflict, you may be mildly interested about how it turns out. You might want to hear more out of curiosity and watch the drama unfold.
- If you've had a similar conflict and it worked out well, your interest

would increase. You may want to hear more and root for them to come up with the right resolution (yours!). You may even find the urge to jump in and say, "My spouse and I had the same problem once and here's what we did."

- If you had a similar conflict and it didn't work out well, your interest may take a different turn. You may want to hear more to see if they handle it differently (better) than you did.

That's the interesting thing about conflict. No matter what level of interest you have, the urge to learn what happens next is almost irresistible. It is nearly impossible to be indifferent when witnessing a conflict.

Resolving conflicts is how we make decisions. Major decisions or minor decisions – it doesn't matter. We are not machines that take in reams of data, process it and make decisions based solely on the evidence. We are nuanced. We are emotional. We think about implications. We debate with ourselves. It is how we decide what to do.

The Universal Hook

> Conflict is to storytelling what sound is to music.
>
> *Robert McKee*
> *Author & Screenwriting Teacher*

Whether it's observing a couple in an airport, considering suppliers for a big project, or deciding what to have for dinner tonight, there is one – and *only* one – hook that gets us every time: conflict.

I'm not talking about tricks that break through the clutter. This is not about icebreakers or jingles or catchy slogans that capture interest for a few seconds then blend into the general background noise. I'm talking about a way to encourage an audience to sit up and give serious consideration to a proposal. I'm talking about using conflict in your presentation to engage your audience and keep it engaged.

> In life we prefer an absence of conflict. In what we read [or watch or listen to], an absence of conflict means an absence of stimulation. Few things are as boring as listening to uncontested testimony in a courtroom. Few things are as interesting as a courtroom clash…dramatic conflict has been the basis of stories from the beginning of time.
>
> *Sol Stein*
> *Author & Playwright*

You may be saying to yourself: "Wait a minute. The last thing I want to do is remind people how complicated their lives are. I want them to forget their problems and go along with my recommendations."

I had the same thought when I investigated the story structure for business presentations. Then I thought about it. Had I ever forgotten my cares when making a serious decision? Had I ever not weighed conflicting interests when making such decisions? Had I ever been so dazzled by a presentation that I suspended all thinking? If I hadn't, why should my audience?

Conflict may be unpleasant in our own lives, but it's not unpleasant to consider it from a safe distance. We willingly pay to watch conflicts every time we go to the movies, watch a game, or read a newspaper. *Our* conflicts are painful – *other* people's conflicts are entertaining.

Conflicts are not objections. They are presentation stimulants. They should be embraced and featured prominently. Especially when you have a means of ultimately resolving those conflicts.

Using Conflict as the Organizing Scheme of Your Presentation

Every presentation has an organizing scheme: the effort the presenter puts into making his or her message understandable to the audience.

Cognitive research and the human instincts make it clear that organizing a message around the facts is a recipe for disinterest. There is an alternative scheme: ask yourself, "What conflicts must be resolved in order to influence the audience to accept my proposal?"

This approach allows the presenter to examine a business case in a way that mirrors how the audience thinks. If a proposition is offered, most people begin weighing the pros and cons. They set up an informal scale and begin weighing options. In the Customer Service example, the message is about "sustainability." The audience may have dozens of sustainability stories. Some of those stories will support the presenter's ideas – others may contradict the story. It doesn't matter. By acknowledging that the audience has conflicts, the exchange becomes richer.

How do you make the switch to conflict-based presentations? There are four steps:

1. *Review the premise.* The premise is a statement of what the story is about and what it does for the audience. Look deeper though, and you'll find conflicts. Possible gains requiring sacrifices, relief from current burdens but the possibility of future ones.

Organizing Your Presentation Around Conflict

1. Review the premise.
2. Apply the "Yeah but..." protocol.
3. Discover the common thread.
4. Identify the core conflict.

2. *Apply the "Yeah but..." protocol.* Have you worked with someone who whenever a new idea was raised said, "Yeah, but...we've already tried that," or "that won't work," or "management will never support it." Irritating, right? But, in a way, that person is a "conflict machine." He or she is framing the issue in terms of the conflicts that must be resolved in order for action to take place.

3. *Discover the common thread.* In many situations, the conflicts the audience brings to the presentation are no more than individual frames (financial, human resources, operations, etc.). Yet the audience members have common interests: to do what's best for the organization. If they're customers, it's to realize the best values. If they're contractors, it's to provide the best services. Frames can be overridden by a common thread – the larger good.

4. *Identify the **Core Conflict**.* No matter how complex great stories can become, they can always be boiled down to a fundamental core conflict – man vs. nature, lovers vs. disapproving families, etc. Many business presentations fail because the presenter is unable or unwilling to boil what has to be said into a compelling core conflict.

As a species, we don't have an unlimited number of stories – but we do have an unlimited number of ways to tell them. A wag once said that there are only seven stories and Hollywood keeps telling them over and over again.

In the business world, seven might be a generous estimate.

Does that mean you're doomed to tell the same story over and over again? Not at all. There is fertile ground for discovering resonance. Is business ever going to tire of hearing ways to increase profits without alienating customers? Will the non-profit sector become bored hearing about ways to funnel more funds to beneficiaries while maintaining the ability to raise funds and manage grants? Will government ever lose interest in improving enforcement while following their legal mandates? Examination of these conflicts is only boring if the stories are told badly.

Go to the Storyboard

Using the storyboard to continue the Customer Service example, the presenter can boil the story down to one core conflict – reduce wait time vs. maintain current cost structure.

The core conflict is self-inflicted. The budget restrictions are having a negative impact on the overall operation – and time is running out. If the organization can't find a way to reduce wait time without increasing costs, then there is no story.

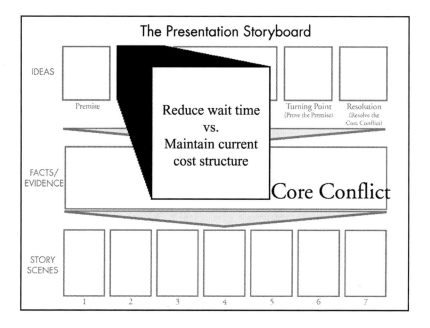

Identifying the core conflict is the most important part of the story development process. That's because conflict resonates and allows the audience to consider the business issue through the structure of a story – what stands between the current situation and a successful outcome.

To develop and test the core conflict of your presentation, apply the "yeah, but..." protocol to isolate the real problem and then look for the common thread that will tie the expectations of the audience to your resolution.

Chapter 9
Using Suspense and Tension to Hold Interest

If you have been successful in making the conflict apparent to your audience, why not resolve it? Why not bring your presentation to a dramatic close by offering your Resolution right then and there?

Because every good story includes an element of suspense – something that stretches the core conflict and provides an edge so that the listeners really want to see what happens next. This chapter examines the sources of tension in a business presentation, and explains how to build tension into your storyline.

The Audience May Not Want a Resolution Yet

People have a natural inclination to relate a story or presentation to their own stories and conflicts. "What's similar? What's different? Where do I fit into this conflict? What should I do?"

People want to resolve the conflict of a story themselves, even if they aren't sure of the answers – to become, in a sense, a co-author. As the characters proceed through the action, readers and listeners think, "I would do this now," or "I wouldn't go in there for the all the money in the world." People allow the author to decide the final resolution – but usually won't be happy if the ending is too different from what they had in mind.

That level of engagement is exactly what a storyteller or presenter wants. The trick is to string people along

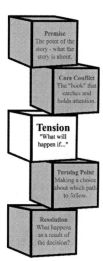

just far enough to keep them engaged without going too far and losing them. Professional writers and teachers have one word for this – *tension.*

Where Does Tension Come From?

Stretching the Truth

Here's how the playwright and editor Sol Stein describes the use of tension: "The word tension is derived from the Latin *tendere*, meaning 'to stretch.' Tension is stretching out. Think of stretching a rubber band more and more. If you stretch it too far, it will break... Tension produces instantaneous anxiety, and the reader finds it delicious."

Tension does not have to come from some dramatic action or shock. Your goal should be to motivate people to think about the core conflict, and to examine as many implications of that conflict as possible. From that point, they should develop a sense of urgency to at least consider a course of action.

Storytellers have many terms for this technique. You may have heard of the "snowball effect" and the "law of unintended consequences." Tension is built in a story or presentation by considering the implications of resolving or not resolving conflict. When a conflict is described, people start to review the implications. Here is an example:

> Chris has just been diagnosed as borderline diabetic. The doctor has said that if there is not true change in eating habits and a weight reduction, Chris may have to begin insulin therapy within two years. Chris' job includes regular entertainment for clients – which means big meals. Chris makes a great living, loves the job, and considers many of the clients to be friends.

The conflict is apparent: a healthy lifestyle vs. job expectations. Evaluating the conflict means thinking about the implications. If Chris doesn't make some changes soon, then there is a significant health risk. At the same time, a dramatic diet and lifestyle change may have a negative impact on Chris' job.

Thinking through the implications creates a sense of urgency as people wrestle with a conflict. What may seem unimportant can become critical when all the dimensions are considered.

Implications. Consequences. Different angles. That is how good storytellers maintain interest and bring the story forward. The **7-Slide Solution™** uses the same structure: to open up the core conflict and lay it out on the table. Show the impact if the conflict is not resolved. Create an obstacle course to success and then lead your audience through the obstacles. By examining consequences, you create the emotional climate that drives your story forward and moves the audience to consider change.

Building Tension

The next time you prepare a presentation, consider how these tension-building techniques will strengthen your premise, create urgency around the core conflict, and move the story forward.

1. *Danger on the horizon.* Nothing drives home the urgency of a conflict more than the threat to the audience's well-being. "Is our present our future? Or is our future something very different?" Describing a threat in the not-too-distant future can frame a core conflict in a new way and create positive tension.

2. *Time and urgency.* For many people, a lack of time is the number one source of stress. For example, if the group has conditioned itself to believe that the negative implications of a conflict won't be felt for years, then provide data to demonstrate how those implications will be felt in a matter of months.

3. *A surprise event.* This is an occurrence either inside or outside of the organization that the audience may not know about. For example, there could be new software about to be released that could give the competition a substantial advantage "if we don't act now."

More Information About The Customer Service Example

The manager of the Customer Service department has reviewed business conditions and discovered two major insights:

First, the company has approximately $300 million in service contract renewals that are due in the next 18 months.

Second, competing customer service providers have begun to advertise their advantages - low wait times and high satisfaction levels. These providers are actively soliciting the company's business.

Building Tension

1. Danger on the Horizon
2. Time and Urgency
3. A Surprise Event
4. A Rapidly Closing Environment

4. *A rapidly closing environment.* This technique relies on the facts to make a credible business case that the options will be even more limited if the audience doesn't act quickly. Technological advances, low cost

competition, and powerful social or economic influences can all create a sense of claustrophobia – the walls may be closing in while action is delayed.

Go to the Storyboard

Returning to the storyboard for the Customer Service example the presenter lists the points that will add tension to the core conflict. These are the issues that should keep the audience awake at night. The most critical is that $300 million in contract renewals is at stake if management does not respond quickly.

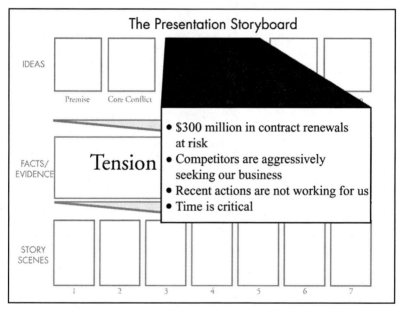

As you plan a business story, you generally have a pretty good sense of how to resolve the core conflict – how to move the current situation into a new direction. But presenting the resolution too soon can disengage the audience – people want to examine the implications and figure out how the story will end. By using tension within the presentation, you can create some suspense, heighten the resonance of your premise, and give your listeners the chance to "mull things over" before steering them toward the turning point. Because every story has a moment of truth.

Chapter 10
The Turning Point

Every good story has momentum: a desire to see what comes next. This momentum is created through a core conflict that is "stretched" to create tension and suspense. If the story is well told, then the audience is engaged in the tension and willing to continue the ride – *for a while.* Ultimately, however, the audience will want some relief.

This chapter explains how you can apply the power of a good storyteller to bring a business presentation to a climax – and offer relief to the tension.

THE POWER OF THE STORYTELLER

A good story manipulates its audience in order to hold attention. The storyteller is afforded the right to create a situation, lead listeners through it, and determine how it will end. We allow the storyteller to play with our emotions – to confront us with conflict and tease us with tension. We don't mind this manipulation one bit. In fact, we work to make a story our own by relating it to our own experience.

With power comes responsibility. A primary responsibility of a good storyteller is to relieve the tension that has been created throughout the story. Think of an *Indiana Jones* movie that builds tension event after tension event (snakes, boulders, Nazis, etc.): if the movie never reaches a conclusion, you would eventually tire of the ride and want to get off.

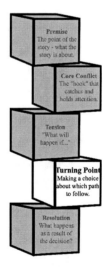

Many business presentations seem to create tension in the hope that *someone else* will ultimately relieve it. These presentations provide slide after slide of statistics that create a picture of dire possibilities (or rosy projections), but they never offer relief. Whether this is done from fear of "sticking their necks out" or an absence of clear ideas is hard to say, but the net effect is profound disappointment and, sometimes, anger.

THE PRESENTATION "TRANQUILIZER"

Here is a short story – how can the tension be relieved?

Bob is an up-and-coming junior executive in a large firm. He has recently been promoted to a new department (his third promotion in two years). The Vice-President in charge of his function has told him, off the record, that if he receives a positive performance review from the department head, he can expect another promotion within the year. "Keep an eye on things," the VP says, "let me know what you observe – positive or negative."

Ron, a veteran employee of the company who is two years from retirement, runs the new department. Ron helps Bob out in the early going. But in Bob's opinion, Ron is "asleep at the switch." He has more or less turned day-to-day operations over to younger staffers. Bob believes that these staffers are running roughshod over the department. He has observed expense account abuses, people leaving early, inappropriate behavior with administrative staff, and a host of other problems.

At first, Bob sees a great opportunity to further his career: simply clean up the mess and let the VP know about it. But as time goes on, he realizes it's not that easy. "Ron could lose his job" he thinks, "and some pension benefits. Even if he doesn't lose his job, Ron will conduct my performance review – and a bad review could hold me back from my next promotion." He thinks further, "I could go to Ron and turn the staffers in – but I don't want to be a 'snitch.' I could approach the staffers directly, but I'm new in the department and lack credibility. I could go to the VP and turn the whole bunch in – but she'll probably just buck it back to Ron."

In this story, Bob faces the conflict of "fix the department vs. lie low and hope to get out soon." He has considered implications to his reputation, Ron's future, and his credibility. Now, Bob's story is at the turning point. The business practices of the department conflict with what he thinks is right, but he has personal, professional, and emotional reasons that hold him back from resolving the conflict. How can the tension be relieved?

The answer can be summed up in three words – *Make a decision.*

Sometimes called the moment of truth, or the climax, or the turning point, good stories always have a point where a character must make a decision.

Decision = Relief

Screenwriting teacher Robert McKee calls the turning point the "obligatory" scene: "…without it, you have no story. Until you have it, your characters wait like suffering patients praying for a cure." Replace "characters" with "business colleagues" in that quote and you get a picture of the importance of proposing a decision in your **7-Slide Solution™** business presentation.

HOLD OFF ON THE SOLUTION JUST A LITTLE BIT LONGER

If you think about your favorite story, the most powerful scene is usually not the final scene – it's the scene just before the end. The scene where the lead character is frozen for a moment and faced with a choice. The scene where we, as the audience, root for the character to make the right choice. The scene that brings the story together and then plunges us into the consequences of the choice.

I believe that a turning point should be built into your business presentations. If you have successfully identified the core conflict, if you have examined the implications of not resolving that conflict, why not suspend your audience for one additional moment by offering a choice, and then lead the audience to the resolution?

This may seem a bit manipulative. After all, you know the solution you want to recommend, so why not just go for it?

You could do that, but there is no real need to rush the decision. The turning point of the presentation gives people time to think – to formulate preliminary solutions of their own.

CHARACTERISTICS OF A COMPELLING TURNING POINT

What makes a compelling turning point or climax?

1. *Relieve the tension.* Offer a light at the end of the tunnel. You can use a phrase like "The way forward is clear…" or "A solution is possible …" This allows the audience to sit back, take a breath, and prepare for your solution.

2. *Offer a choice.* This is the most important part of the turning point. Just as a storyteller has a moment of truth where the lead character must decide, your presentation should put the choices squarely in front of the audience.

3. *Examine the consequences of action or inaction.* Most of these consequences can be reiterated from the tension you built early in the story.

It is at the turning point that the audience should recognize that the premise has been proved and a resolution can be considered.

GO TO THE STORYBOARD

Returning to the storyboard for the presentation in the Customer Service example, the presenter is ready to state the turning point. As in many business presentations, the choice offered is between maintaining the status quo or considering another way.

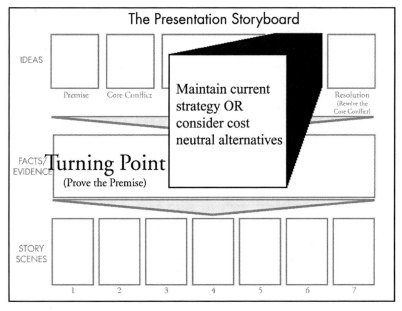

The turning point of your presentation relieves the tension created through conflict and consequences, but continues the momentum of the story. It creates a desire to see what comes next by placing a choice before the audience. A choice for which you will show consequences.

Chapter 11
Resolution: Closing The Loop

You have taken your audience on a ride: you posed a compelling premise and your audience wanted to learn more.

You identified a core conflict that keeps the audience up at night. You created the interest.

You increased the urgency of that interest by exploring the implications of *not* resolving the core conflict. This created tension for your audience and maintained the interest to see what happens next.

When the tension became intense, you relieved it by offering a choice to follow one path or another.

This is where successful business presentations diverge from novels, films, or stories. Traditional story-tellers are allowed to "play God." *They* determine what choices are made and how things turn out. The audience is passive and leaves it up to the author to bring the story to a satisfying conclusion.

Not so in business presentations. Organizational resources, politics, and power structures come into play. In most organizations, consensus is essential to making things work. "Playing God" won't cut it. But – you must be able to *offer* a resolution to your business story.

This chapter examines what resolution is in relation to the core conflict. This chapter also describes the difference between resolution and solution – they are not the same and do not have the same function within a

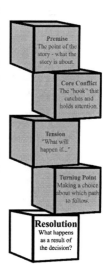

presentation. Then, this chapter reviews the consequences of action and inaction on the part of your audience – deciding to do nothing is a decision, and the impact of that decision must be understood by the audience members before they proceed. In terms of closing the story, this chapter looks at what it takes to rest your case. The chapter concludes with a look at the storyboard.

What Is Resolution?

The turning point of a story or presentation demands a decision. Audiences demand to know how that decision turns out. That's why so many stories include a brief scene that wraps up the loose ends and explains how things turn out.

Imagine a film where the hero decides to risk his life to save a loved one. How would you feel if you never knew whether he lived or died? Or, a young woman decides to give up a life of wealth and privilege to spend her life with her poor, but honest, lover. Would you be satisfied if you didn't get a glimpse of how her life turned out?

There are four guidelines you can follow to provide effective resolution:

1. *Resolve the core conflict.* This is the primary function of the resolution.
2. *Recognize the difference between <u>resolution</u> and solution.* There is a difference, and it's an important one.
3. *Reveal the consequences of action <u>and</u> inaction.* Show what can happen, good and bad.
4. *Finish early and rest your case.* Sooner or later, the jury closes the story.

First and Foremost, <u>Resolve</u> the Core Conflict

Resolve the Core Conflict

1. Remind them of the core conflict
2. Don't try to change the world
3. Let them have their cake and eat it, too
4. Extend, don't defend

What makes any story interesting is conflict. Resistance. Opposition. Walking away without resolving that conflict is unacceptable. The audience won't allow it. What is true of a successful story is true of a successful business presentation.

You may think that the conflict was so well established in the presentation that only an idiot would have lost track of it, but that's not the case. It doesn't hurt to remind your audience of the conflict you want to resolve. This can be a simple statement like, "As I said earlier, our challenge is deciding whether to pursue sustainable growth or short-term margin enhancement." A little refresher can keep people (including you) on track.

A successful resolution of a business story does not – generally – call for a change in the existing world order. That is, don't build the core conflict into a situation that cannot be resolved. Your resolution should not presume that a powerful competitor will suddenly vanish from the face of the earth, or that your recommendation will instantly overturn government regulations. Design your premise to be achievable, and build the conflict and tension toward that goal. Don't offer a resolution that cannot be realized.

The best resolutions are the ones that allow the audience to "have their cake and eat it, too." It's not always possible, but if you can find a way to let the audience realize some satisfaction from both sides of the conflict (for example, some sustainable growth and some margin enhancement), then I can guarantee that your proposal will receive positive attention.

Finally, be prepared to encounter resistance to your resolution. Your audience thinks about conflicts all day long. Extend an invitation to generate alternatives. Don't become defensive.

Recognize the Difference Between <u>R</u>esolution and Solution

Many presenters think that a detailed action plan is the resolution of a core conflict. I believe this is overkill. I also believe that too much detail can seriously harm an otherwise compelling business story.

Governments issue resolutions to express their commitment to make changes. People make New Year's resolutions to express their intentions to change bad habits or to do good work. Competitors test each other's resolve in order to gauge each other's strengths.

Students calculate solutions to math problems. Engineers provide IT solutions to common business problems. There are cleaning solutions, chemical solutions, and moral solutions.

An Example of the 7-Slide Solution™ in Action

As part of the investigation into the problems faced by the Customer Service Department, the manager has learned…

- The department is overspending in capital investment
- Savings can be realized if investments are spread over 2 - 3 years
- Lots of capacity in the Western Call Center is not used
- There have been several requests to sub-let space in the Western call center

Resolutions are commitments. Solutions are answers. People can resolve to change without really knowing how they will do it. A solution is the work plan. A resolution is the vision.

The resolution of a business story can be conceptual. For example, "Establish realistic and sustainable growth targets in light of current margin pressures." A solution must be specific: "Grow revenue 8% per year for the next 5 years, while increasing margin 1% a year."

Resolutions can be discussed and expanded. Solutions can be resisted and opposed.

Does that mean you shouldn't have a detailed plan if someone asks for it? Absolutely not. Keep the plan in reserve, but don't make it part of the storyline.

Reveal the Consequences of Action and Inaction

The turning point of a presentation offers a choice – a fork in the road. Often (though not always), the choice is to maintain the status quo or consider something significantly different.

Naturally, the presenter prefers one direction to the other. A common mistake presenters make is to provide only the benefits of the preferred path, while ignoring the other.

A good resolution examines the consequences of both possible avenues. If the presenter wants to maintain the status quo, the benefits of the present situation are highlighted and the risks of change are forewarned. If change is the objective, then the dangers of complacency are emphasized, while the opportunities of the new path are highlighted.

This examination of action and inaction can tip the balance of undecided members of your audience by clearly comparing and/or contrasting competing outcomes.

Rest Your Case

When to Rest Your Case

1. You have nothing left to add
2. The audience seems to approve
3. You sense that any more will simply overload the story
4. Finish early

I have always liked the legal term "rest" ("The prosecution rests," "I rest my case"). It conveys a sense of "I've done all I can do – it's up to you, the jury, to decide." It communicates a sense of confidence that the case has been well made. It also sends a message of trust to the jury – "You can take it from here."

Too many presenters lack the confidence to rest their case. They constantly add "one more thing." Or they ask the dumbest question any presenter can ask. What's that question? "Are there any questions?" Think about it: is there a clearer indication that a presenter lacks confidence in his or her story than by asking that question? If people have questions, they'll ask them – unsolicited. If they don't, asking the dumbest question won't suddenly motivate them to formulate their own. The best advice…

- Plan your story to include exactly what you want to say and recognize, *before* you begin the presentation, that that is *all* you want to say.
- Accept the implied approval of the audience and ask for agreement in principle.
- Realize that including more examples will contribute to "information overload."
- Shut up and never forget the value of finishing your presentation early.

The audience will take it from there.

Go to the Storyboard

The storyline is almost complete. The only step remaining is to define the resolution scene in the Customer Service example.

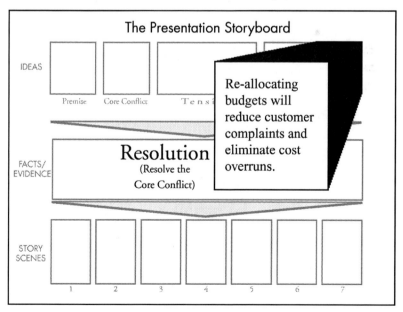

The Presentation Storyboard

IDEAS

Premise   Core Conflict   Tension

FACTS/ EVIDENCE

Resolution
(Resolve the
Core Conflict)

Re-allocating budgets will reduce customer complaints and eliminate cost overruns.

STORY SCENES

1   2   3   4   5   6   7

This statement resolved the core conflict: the department is faced with increasing complaints but must exist within strict budget guidelines. This resolution is not the solution – it does not specify how the budget will be re-allocated. The audience will surely ask and that's fine. I can specify "how" in an additional story.

Here is how the top line of the storyboard looks with all the story components completed.

The Presentation Storyboard

IDEAS	Avoid customer defections by reducing wait time without increasing budgets.	Reduce wait time vs. Maintain current cost structure	• $300 million in contract renewals at risk • Competitors are aggressively seeking our business • Recent actions are not working for us • Time is critical	Maintain current strategy OR consider cost neutral alternatives	Re-allocating budgets will reduce customer complaints and eliminate cost overruns
	Premise	Core Conflict	T e n s i o n	Turning Point (Prove the Premise)	Resolution (Resolve the Core Conflict)

The resolution of the story is the scene where the storyteller – or business presenter – resolves the core conflict for the audience. The tension was relieved at the turning point, but the resolution closes the loop. In order to create a successful resolution, the presenter must be aware of the difference between resolution and solution. The presenter must also be able to describe the consequences of action and inaction. When the resolution has been described to the audience, the presenter can rest the case.

Now that the storyline is ready, the next step is to determine the facts that best support the story.

The Story Platform

The most powerful communication device on earth is deceptively simple.

- It starts with a premise that resonates both intellectually and emotionally with the audience.
- Then, it creates a "hook" by identifying a core conflict that, if resolved, will ease the anxieties of the audience.
- Stories proceed to stretch the core conflict by creating tension through an examination of possible consequences and implications.

- The tension is relieved, as tension always is, when someone *decides* to do something. This is the turning point.
- The story ends with a resolution of the core conflict and a picture of how things can be.

Five simple steps that have influenced mankind in more ways than anyone can count.

Five simple steps that can revolutionize the way you communicate on the job, at church, or anywhere else where you need to persuade people to think differently.

Chapter 12
What About The Facts?

Cognitive science is clear: ***People think in ideas, not facts.*** And I believe stories are the most powerful way to communicate ideas.

In order to make business decisions, professionals need to review the key facts that support important ideas. This chapter shows you how to integrate facts into your business story: what to put in, and what to leave out. The chapter also takes a look at how people make decisions, based on the facts, and how they interpret facts within the scope of a story. Then, the chapter gives you specific tips about using facts in the storyboard.

The information revolution of the 1980's and 1990's changed forever the way organizations look at themselves. Not surprisingly, as the cost of data processing declined, the amount of data collected exploded.

Whether it is janitorial work or mergers and acquisitions, workers at every level of an organization are no longer required to simply perform the tasks associated with their jobs. They are also expected to analyze processes, report results and share insights with the rest of the organization. Virtually every worker is, at least part of the time, an information worker. Managers within each function become intimately involved with their particular set of data. Typically, each function believes that its data are among the most vital to the health of the organization. In a word, many become *zealots*.

On the one hand, managers must be able to dig so deeply into functional data that the answer to any question is at their fingertips. On the other hand, they must be able to step back from the data and assume another role – communicator.

Organizations don't ask scientists to sell products. They don't ask sales people to conduct experiments. Yet those functional distinctions break down in the day-to-day world of conducting business. Managers are expected to be *both* "scientist and salesman." A constant challenge that information workers (i.e. all of us) face is that it is very difficult to do both.

What to Put in, What to Leave Out

Statistics as "Social Products"

We sometimes talk about statistics as though they are facts that simply exist, like rocks, completely independent of people, and that people gather statistics much as rock collectors pick up stones. This is wrong. All statistics are created through people's actions: people have to decide what to count and how to count it, people have to do the counting and other calculations, and people have to interpret the resulting statistics, to decide what the numbers mean. All statistics are social products, the results of people's efforts.

Joel Best
Damned Lies and Statistics

As we approach any important presentation, we are faced with a core conflict: the need to include enough data to be credible versus the requirement to be concise and interesting to an audience.

If too much data is included, the perception may arise that the presenter is too focused on the details and can't see the big picture. If too little data is included, the presenter may be written off as a lightweight.

In an effort to resolve this conflict, some presenters end up by compromising the integrity of the presentation. They create visuals for virtually every fact that may impact the message. Then, they determine they can "skip over" slides if the audience seems disinterested.

The problem is that the audience is unaware of what is "skipable" information and what is not. The audience relies on the presenter to make the decisions about what's important and what's not. As Voltaire said, "The best way to be boring is to leave nothing out."

"Satisficing"

What is the right balance?

All of us like to think that we are objective decision makers who collect all available data, weigh all the alternatives, prioritize and make the *optimum* decision based on the data available.

The truth is something different. In 1955, economist H.A. Simon coined the word *"satisficing."* The *Complete Problem Solver* by John R. Hayes describes the concept like this:

> "The satisficing method requires the decision maker to identify the *worst* value he is willing to accept for each of the attributes [that comprise a decision]. He then considers all of the alternatives in

order, rejecting any alternatives which fall below the minimal values of the attributes, and accepting the *first* alternative which meets all of the minimal values." [Italics are mine]

In other words, for most decisions, we don't seek to realize the best result – we seek to realize the least objectionable result. Once we've reached that minimum level of satisfaction, we stop looking for alternatives and make a decision. Here's an example. A couple's dream house includes more than 20 features, such as a luxury master bath and a Viking range in the kitchen. After shopping for some time, the couple realizes that obtaining all 20 of their dream features may be unreasonable, and they find a house that includes 14 of their dream amenities. Rather than prolong their search, they satisfice and give up on some of their dream features.

As you consider the data to include in your presentation, don't think about the amount needed to make an *optimal* decision – think about the minimum amount needed to make an *acceptable* decision. More often than not, that will be enough to help your audience decide.

The Understanding Hierarchy

We have learned from cognitive science that we are not particularly good at grasping and holding on to facts unless they are related to bigger ideas.

Our ability to comprehend information can be ranked hierarchically. The most memorable concepts are basic premises: "Haste makes waste," "There's no place like home," "What goes around comes around." These are clichés for a reason – these thoughts resonate with people.

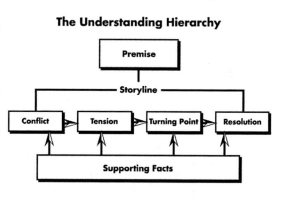

Next in the hierarchy are storylines. They bring the premises to life. *The Tortoise and the Hare, The Wizard of Oz, Macbeth.*

The least memorable items are facts and details. Facts are *only* relevant if they support the scenes of the story. Your favorite movie isn't weighed down with minutia about the characters. Why should your business presentation be weighed down with exacting information about your methodology or how you reached your conclusions? If a fact or statistic can be used to make the core conflict more compelling, or to build tension, or to help your audience choose the right resolution – *then put it in.* Otherwise, leave it out. This is a business presentation, not a peer review for the Nobel Prize.

The Keystone Data Point

The sad truth is that, in all likelihood, your audience will forget the facts and statistics of your presentation *within minutes.* That doesn't mean that facts don't have an impact. They do. But the impact is short-lived.

An effective use of facts is to choose one data point that particularly dramatizes the premise of your story. Think of it as the keystone data point or the "killer statistic." Find a way to repeat this fact throughout the presentation. One theory is that if people hear something three times, they will remember it better. The first time they ask, "What is it?" the second time "What of it … How does it apply to me?" and the final time acts as a reinforcement. It may be challenging to repeat the same statistic three times within a 7-slide presentation, but if it is a really dramatic number, it is worth a try.

Go to the Storyboard

The central section of the storyboard is the place to jot down the facts that will support the story.

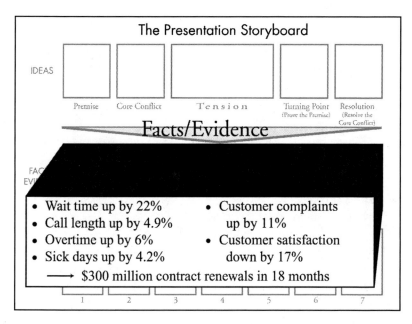

Because the manager framed the customer service story around sustainability – the strongest hand for this audience – most of the facts support that position. In addition, the presenter found a "killer statistic" that will keep the audience waiting to see what will happen next – the $300 million in contract renewals are due in the next 18 months.

Deciding what to bring into a story and what to leave out is a challenge for every storyteller. In a business presentation, if too much data is included, it may appear that the presenter is trying to show off by turning over each stone. However, if too little data is described, the presenter may appear to be unprepared.

To meet the challenge and strike the right balance, include the facts and supporting data that will allow the audience to make an *acceptable* decision. Find a way to use a keystone data point throughout the presentation to drive home your premise and lead the audience to your resolution.

Novelist Cynthia Ozick provides an apt close to this section on ideas, stories and facts. In *We are the Crazy Lady* she writes, "I am not afraid of facts. I welcome facts, but a congeries [collection or compilation] of facts is not equivalent to an idea. This is the essential fallacy of the so-called 'scientific' mind. People who mistake facts for ideas are incomplete thinkers; they are gossips."

Chapter 13
Building the "Scenes" of the Presentation

Before launching PowerPoint® and building the actual presentation, there is one more design task: to complete the blueprint by finishing the storyboard.

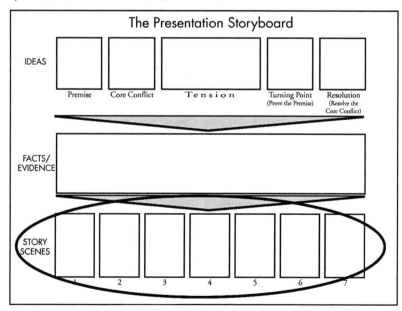

This chapter explains the role of each slide in the **7-Slide Solution™**, and how to use the Story Scenes blocks on the storyboard to complete the draft of the presentation. The critical role of each of the seven slides is reviewed, as well as the practice of using each slide to *show* the story, not to *tell* the story.

Each Slide Has a Unique Role in the 7-Slide Solution™

The Role of Each Slide in the 7-Slide Solution™

Slide 1 – Engagement
Slide 2 – Backstory
Slide 3 – Build tension
Slide 4 – Bring it to a boil
Slide 5 – Offer choice(s)
Slide 6 – Provide resolution
Slide 7 – Set up the "sequel"

Movie directors carefully scout locations and choreograph how each scene will play out and contribute to the overall story. PowerPoint® slides are your locations. They are the visual landscape where your story will play out. Each slide performs a unique role in creating resonance and increasing your ability to persuade the audience.

The first slide may be the most important. It fuels the desire to see what will happen next: a desire that you will build upon throughout the presentation.

When you choose a book in a bookstore, what do you do? If you are like most people, you read the jacket cover summary, browse the index, and maybe read part of the first page. That's when you decide to either buy it or put it back on the shelf. That is the process that your audience members go through as well. They are browsing for something interesting. If they find it, they'll tune in. If they don't, they mentally put you back on the shelf. Slide 1 is where you engage the audience.

If the role of the first slide in any presentation is to bring in the audience, the second slide can be used to describe how the presenter came to this point. Slide 2 – what writers call "backstory" – may not always be necessary (remember, the goal is always 7 slides or *less*). Detailed background data can bog down a story. If you must give a lengthy explanation about how you arrived where you are, you may not have much of a story. However, *some* amount of backstory is almost always necessary. Backstory provides a context so that people can make decisions more clearly. Within the **7-Slide Solution™**, Slide 2 is reserved for backstory.

Tension drives a story forward. The next slide is used to create tension by exploring the consequences and implications of taking or not taking action to address problems and conflicts.

Slide 4 is used to bring the tension to a boiling point. It creates an environment whereby the meeting participants look to you, the presenter, for relief. "Yes," they think, "We have a problem – how do we fix it?"

Tension is relieved only when *someone* makes a decision. That's the turning point. Slide 5 releases the tension valve and offers a choice.

Resolving the core conflict with a "have your cake and eat it too" recommendation is the goal of Slide 6.

The final slide sets up the sequel. It allows the audience to hear more. Go deeper. Verify the facts. Take action.

Seven slides. Each with a specific role to play.

Show, Don't Tell

Although people everywhere communicate and learn through stories, a better term for communicating stories to adults might be story-showing. Adults like to be shown, not told. Adults want just enough information to engage their interest so that they can fill in the blanks.

> Don't say the old lady screamed... bring her on and let her scream.
>
> *Mark Twain*

This is particularly important for people making professional presentations. There is often a great deal of function-specific data in business presentations (market share from marketers, defect rates from manufacturing, "on time and complete" from customer service, etc.). Because the audience does not deal with the data every day, the presenter may feel a need to explain what each statistic means, how it is calculated, and what conclusions should be drawn from it. The result is a tutorial, not a story.

The remedy is to include *only* the data necessary to support your ideas and to *show* rather than tell. For example, here's how an opening scene of a productivity story could be shown instead of told:

Tell	Show
"How have productivity levels changed in the last year?"	A line graph comparing year-to-year productivity gains at the company vs. industry standard.
"Growth has been impressive but is still below industry levels."	Color highlight to show the gap between the company and industry performance; text pull-out of the exact percentage gap.
"Productivity increased by 6%."	The line graph demonstrates the point.
"Here's what we intend to do to improve to industry standard levels."	A tag line that reads "...successes and lessons learned..."

A successful presenter can include all this information on a single slide. Very little dialogue would be required for the audience to get the point.

There are some areas in any presentation where it may be irresistible to do some "telling."

Danger Zones: Temptation to Tell Instead of Show

1. Providing background information
2. Explaining statistics
3. Over-explaining methodology or approach
4. Offering alternatives
5. Giving an action plan

The first is in the backstory or situation analysis section. Many potentially strong presentations have been lost because the presenter felt a need to provide a complete history before getting down to business. Even the best storytellers struggle to achieve the correct balance: too much backstory and the story will lose momentum; too little and it will not make sense. For business presentations, I believe the best advice is to err on the side of too little background. If the audience requires a thorough background briefing, try to do it before the meeting.

Telling the audience about statistics is done with the best of intentions. The presenter works with the data all the time and understands the positive or negative impact a certain figure represents. The presenter also recognizes that the audience doesn't work with the data and may not understand the impact. So the presenter takes a detour and provides some "education." The results can be deadly. For one thing, people don't come to be educated – they come to be informed so they can make better decisions. Secondly, an educational presentation will break the momentum of the story. Rather than explain a statistic, show a comparison – over time or against a benchmark. Another way to avoid telling too much is to offer to explain any statistic if asked.

Laws are like sausages; it is better not to see them being made.
Otto von Bismarck

As presenters, we want our audience to understand that the insights and conclusions we are describing did not come about casually. We want to demonstrate that we are thorough and professional in how we approach our recommendations. This leads to the third "telling" danger zone – over-explaining methodologies and approaches. While few decision makers are willing to make a decision without knowing something about how the research was conducted, the majority wants only enough insight into methodology to help them make the decision. You can offer a written summary of your approach that the audience can review or provide a top line summary and answer questions after the presentation.

The turning point of a story is the "moment of truth" where alternatives are offered and a decision must be made. Some presenters have a "crisis of confidence" when it comes to offering choices. They think, "What if I haven't thought this all the way through?" or "What if the audience has better choices?" When this happens, instead of offering the choice, they explain everything related to the choice – how they came to the conclusion, what factors they considered, or how they eliminated other possible choices. They tell so much about the "how" and "why" of their choice that the choice itself is lost. If there is one area in a storyline where the telling is devastating, it's the turning point. The best advice is: go with your story. If you have a powerful and well-documented story and you believe the choices you are recommending are the best – put them on the table and let the audience respond.

A final danger zone where you might be tempted to tell rather than show is the action plan. Detailed action plans are not always necessary. If an action plan is required, create a document (do not waste a slide) and review the details after the presentation.

Of course, a business meeting is a discussion, and I do not want to imply that a successful presenter stands by silently while the slides do all the work. Keep your explanations of the facts to a minimum, to show and not tell. Use printed materials to summarize your sources and methods and to outline the action plan.

Plan to Finish Early

The straightforward structure of the **7-Slide Solution™** keeps the business story on track. It also helps to keep the presentation on time. Let's face it – we have all attended meetings – even meetings that held our attention – that went far beyond the scheduled time. It's almost common practice.

There are at least three faults with this practice.

In the first place, it's rude – we all have schedules and obligations to meet. Rudeness draws an emotional response – usually anger or, at least, irritation. Since the emotional response to rudeness is immediate, chances are it will trump the other emotions the presenter is trying to tap. The result? The speaker loses the audience.

Expected time and attention spans are related. As an example, most of us are accustomed to 2-hour movies. When a movie starts to run 2 1/2 or 3 hours, we become fidgety. We start to focus more on when it will end than on what's happening on the screen. Presentations are the same. A presentation that goes on and on loses its drama – some people may miss the main point entirely by wondering when the meeting will end.

Finally, a meeting that runs past its allotted time makes the presenter look disorganized. How many presentations have you attended where the presenter rushed to cover the main points communicated while the audience began to pack up and leave?

If you have been allowed one hour for your presentation, plan to deliver it in 50 minutes. This is such a rare occurrence that people are appreciative and are likely to extend the presentation with questions and comments. If they extend, it's great. If you extend, it's an imposition.

As you complete the storyboard – the blueprint of the presentation and the plan to follow as you construct the **7-Slide Solution™** – it is important to follow the architectural doctrine of "form follows function." Each slide has a specific role to play in the story.

As you design each slide, it is important to follow the principle of showing what you mean, not telling with elaborate explanations. Eliminating the "nice to know" information maintains the discipline of the **7-Slide Solution™**, and keeps the presentation on track so that audience members can make a decision. Finally, the design process must be regulated by the clock – plan to finish your presentation early. That ultimate goal – the finish line – will help to maintain a discipline throughout the entire design, construction, and delivery of the presentation.

Part III: Constructing The 7-Slide Business Story

Chapter 14
Some Do's and Don't's for PowerPoint®

It is not the intention of this book to provide graphic design principles – there are plenty of sources you can tap to give you clear ideas on slides and visuals for business presentations. What this chapter provides are some general guidelines for making the most of your PowerPoint® slides.

In the **7-Slide Solution™**, there is only so much space available to describe the conflict and move toward resolution. For that simple reason, each slide should be considered prime real estate. Each slide should be designed according to a "site plan," following the patterns that people have developed whenever they look at an image. This chapter reviews some common practices or conventions for using PowerPoint®, including the use of white space, and gives some tips for developing your own conventions and styles.

Like any tool that mankind has developed, PowerPoint® can be used or abused. PowerPoint® doesn't kill meaning – *people* kill meaning.

Treat Each Slide Like Prime Real Estate

Each PowerPoint® slide starts as an empty lot of valuable real estate just waiting for you to develop it: to plot out what goes where and to optimize the visual experience of your audience. Like an architect, you can optimize the visual space of your slides by combining practicality with aesthetics.

Visual Real Estate

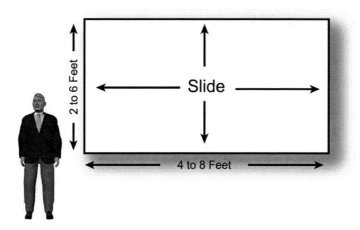

Depending on the size of the room and the quality of projection, you may control a rectangle as large as six feet by eight feet. Put another way: in a seven slide presentation, you may have up to 336 square feet to tell your story. That's bigger than some Manhattan apartments.

As the presenter, you dominate the room and the field of vision of your audience. You control every aspect of the visual field – layout, color, fonts, even when to change the picture. You are the architect, builder, and interior designer all in one.

Design a Site Plan

Builders work from plans. In the same way, you can develop a plan to position the key data points of your message.

Importance can be visually portrayed using a number of graphic devices, but the three most common are:

1. Location: where important messages appear on the visual
2. Size: most important to least important
3. Color: signal importance through color

Like prime real estate, location equals value.

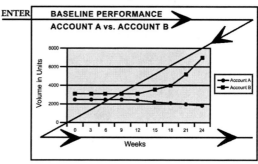

In the western world, we *read* from left to right. When we first look at a page or image, we tend to *scan* it in a "Z" pattern – starting at the top left and moving across the top of the page, then diagonally through the middle, and finishing straight across the bottom. This fundamental pattern is used by print media like newspapers, magazines, and advertisements. The most important information is presented at the top of the page, beginning in the upper-left corner.

Tabloid headlines use different type sizes to shout the editors' most important (or scandalous) stories. Using font sizes that are too large is like building an elegant driveway and not leaving enough room for the house. *Slightly larger* works. Massive is intrusive.

A highlight in another color will draw the eye and frame an important fact or statement. Make sure you know which colors work well together and which do not. A good book or website on graphic design fundamentals includes a color wheel that will help you match colors. Here is one caution about the use of color: according to the Howard Hughes Medical Institute, "Some 10 million American men – fully 7 percent of the male population – either cannot distinguish red from green, or see red and green differently from most people. This is the commonest form of color blindness, but it affects only .4 percent of women."

Content and Design Conventions

A convention is a practice or routine to decide "what goes where." Over the years, business presenters have developed a number of conventions. We expect that each PowerPoint® slide will have a title in a larger font than the body of the text. We expect text to be "bulleted." We are surprised if there are not at least two colors per slide.

Most of these conventions are pretty harmless. However, there are some that have been taken to such extremes that they inhibit rather than enhance effective communications.

Every organization has its own meeting protocols and presentation styles. These standards become so ingrained that meeting leaders and presenters are reluctant to deviate from the norm. Three such conventions that I challenge as a waste of valuable visual real estate are the title slide, the agenda slide, and the objectives slide.

I believe that every slide should be an event. Each slide should be a dramatic scene in the story and point to the next scene so that the audience is anxious to see what happens next. Titles, agendas, and objectives are usually placed at the beginning of a presentation and set a tone of predictability that is the opposite of what the presenter wants to accomplish.

Welcome...

Budget Review Meeting

July 22, 2007

What role does a title slide play? If you are participating in a "Budget Review Meeting," do you need to be told that when you walk into the room? Title slides are lifeless: they are like wallpaper and do not engage the intellect or the emotions. They just sit there until you are ready to begin. The opening is too important to waste on a "dead" visual. Worse than that, they give the audience permission to tune out until the speaker begins.

If it is necessary that you begin with a welcome or title slide, then combine it with specific information, or a question that will engage the audience *before* you start speaking.

Agenda

- Introduction
- 2nd Quarter Results
- 3rd Quarter Projections
- Revisions
- Questions & Answers
- Meeting Close

Agendas are considered a courtesy to the audience. They spell out what topics the audience can expect to discuss and for what length of time. In many cases, agendas have become nothing more than a series of bullet points, without any time frames (lest the group realize that the presenter is, at some point, running late). Once displayed, the agenda is rarely referred to again.

As a courtesy to the audience, announce when the meeting will close ("We will be finished at three o'clock sharp!"). Make sure that you can deliver your story *before* that time – if you have 30 minutes to give your presentation, make every effort to conclude in 20 minutes.

If you absolutely must have an agenda, then either send it before the meeting or have one printed and waiting on the table for each attendee. Don't waste good visual real estate with an image as unexciting as an agenda.

Objectives are another over-used convention, and one that seems to benefit the presenter rather than the audience. Like the agenda, objectives slides are shown early in the presentation and never referred to again – so only those people with photographic memories can evaluate whether the objectives were achieved.

The Tyranny of White Space

In the early days of PowerPoint®, presenters packed as much information onto each slide as they could. Presenters often apologized for particularly busy slides, calling them "eye charts." There was a rightful (and righteous) rebellion against this and people began to emphasize the need for extensive "white space" on each slide.

Although white space is important in advertising where people are glancing through a magazine or surfing channels, presentation visuals should be stimulating and comprehensive – "busyness" is not the issue when it comes to understanding visuals.

People have amazing scanning abilities (350 megabytes per second). We can find our destinations using highly detailed maps. We can look at the ceiling of the Sistine Chapel and appreciate its beauty. We can look through the stock tables and determine how our investments are doing. So why do we design PowerPoint® slides to insultingly simplistic levels? Why inflate the number of slides so that the presentation is a long series of brief points, resembling an old-time silent movie – jerky and hard to follow?

"Simpleness is another aesthetic preference, not an information display strategy, not a guide to clarity. What we seek instead is a rich texture of data, a comparative context, an understanding of complexity revealed with an economy of means."

Edward R. Tufte
Envisioning Information

Somewhere, someone read George Miller's finding that people can only hold seven pieces of information in short term memory and ran with it. This someone decreed that every visual should only have seven data points. PowerPoint® automated the convention and made "bulleting" a global communication standard. It's true that a few words on a slide are easier to hold in short-term memory than more words. So what? If the message isn't important or memorable, short-term memory will discard it.

We have come to think of a PowerPoint® presentation as a fast-moving (click, click, click), visually unchallenging show. We expect to see each slide for a few seconds before it is quickly replaced by the next one. Simple slides are easy to comprehend because they don't *say* anything. They fail to challenge the intellect or elicit much emotion.

Develop Your Own Design Conventions

How do you break these conventions? Develop some new conventions of your own.

First, use seven slides or less for *every* presentation. Using fewer slides forces you to think about the content of the visual field you are presenting. This discipline will allow you to become a better storyteller by marrying your storyline to the visual representations.

Don't think that you must explain every element of a slide. Project it. Remain silent and let the audience drink it in. Allow the data to act as a backdrop to support what you say. Whatever you do, *please* never read from the slide.

Make a conscious effort to keep each visual displayed for a longer period of time. If you normally display a slide for 30 seconds, for example, make an effort to project each slide for 2.5 or 3 *minutes*. This will accomplish two things:

1. It will encourage you to design each visual for maximum impact. The audience will be looking at it for a long time, so it better be interesting.

Make Slides Informative, Not Decorative

1. Use seven slides or less for every presentation
2. Show, don't tell
3. Project each slide for times longer that your audience expects
4. Verbally bring the audience's attention to one area of the slide, and then another

---

Interesting doesn't mean lots of white space. It means making the visual say what you want it to say.

2. It will signal to the audience that your slides aren't simply decoration but are meant to be informative – so pay attention!

Have you ever taken an audio tour at a museum – those headsets where you plug in a number and the curator explains what you're looking at? These guides analyze the picture in discrete sections and explain each element in detail. You can do the same by verbally calling attention to a particular section of your slide. Just as a museum guide can help you focus on a particular aspect of a painting, you can help your audience to do the same. The picture does not have to speak for itself if you are there to interpret it.

Don't worry about putting too much information on a slide – concern yourself with putting too little *meaningful information* on a slide.

Using seven (or less) informative visuals, and projecting them long enough so that the audience can understand the message and discuss the key points, is a far better alternative than the incessant clicking of 20 or 30 slides, which are forgotten almost as quickly as they are projected.

So, how do you design such a slide?

Slide design should follow the scene structure:

1. Plant a question
2. Evoke an emotion
3. Answer the question
4. Move the story forward

Reserve the prime real estate of your presentation to plant a question in the minds of the audience. Does it actually have to be a question? No, there are other ways:

1. *A claim.* This plants questions relating to the credibility of the presenter. "Is that true?" "Can he really deliver?" If you are prepared to back up your claim and cement your credibility by answering those questions, then you have used the real estate well.
2. *A concept, theory or hypothesis.* This poses questions like, "How does this compare to my theory?" "How does this compare to what we are already doing?" If it's a good concept, then "How do I learn more?"
3. *A challenge.* This raises the question, "Are we up to it?"
4. *A proposition or "deal."* This prompts questions like "Can you show me how?" or "Where do we get the resources?"

5. *Simple Truth.* The blindingly obvious can also generate questions like "That's true for others, but is it true for us?" or "Can this be true – it seems so simple?"

All of these techniques raise questions in the minds of the audience. If you are prepared to explore those questions and answer them, then you have the start of a successful visual.

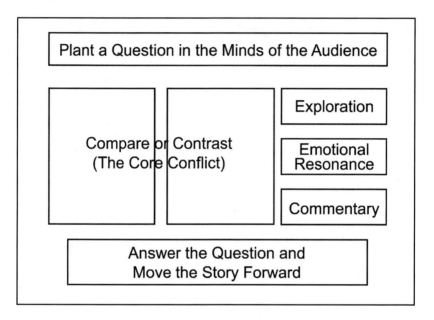

Decisions are generally made by resolving conflict. Comparing and contrasting information is one way conflicts are presented and ultimately resolved. For that reason, allocate your next most valuable real estate within the diagonal eye track showing side-by-side charts, or graphs, or data that encourage the audience to make comparisons and/or contrast situations.

People *hate* unanswered questions. They will go looking for an answer if one is not provided. That's why you can use the least valuable real estate for the answer to the question you planted, as well as the link to the next slide to move the story forward.

Because you will answer the questions that you've raised, you can allocate the bottom line of the eye track to that function. This can also be the space where you move the story forward and connect to the next slide.

Here's an example of a slide following these conventions.

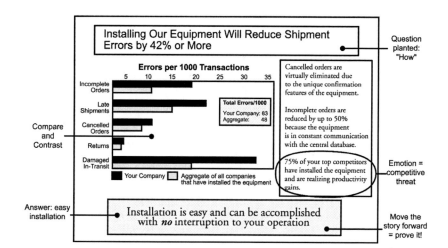

At first glance, that slide may appear busy. I would argue that it is not.

1. The image on this page is about 8.25 square inches. You may have as much as 48 *square feet* to project it. Murals, tapestries, and panoramas pack substantially more imagery in less space.

2. Most people are able to scan this entire visual in one sweep and are then able to fill in the gaps they missed.

3. This is one of only seven slides. If you're planning a 30-minute presentation, each visual should be projected for an average of 4 1/2 minutes. That is plenty of time for the audience to look at, absorb, and comprehend your message.

4. The design follows the "eye track," like the front page of the newspaper.

5. It is not a stand-alone image. It has a presenter (you) to lead the group through it.

Am I saying that once you have developed your design conventions that *each and every* slide must look exactly the same? Of course not. But marrying the message of a good scene with visual conventions will make your story that much more persuasive.

Adult Peek-a-Boo: Bullets and Builds

The example slide does not include any short, one or two word bullets. That's because I believe that bullets have become a crutch to support poor visual design. Intended to focus the attention of the audience on a few key words or phrases, bullets replace communication with shortened versions of the truth. As Gordon Shaw of 3M said in the *Harvard Business Review*, "[We are] genially tricking ourselves into supposing that we have planned when, in fact, we've only listed some good things to do."

This is exacerbated by the practice of building slides by revealing each bullet one at a time. It's almost as if presenters are playing "peek-a-boo" with their audiences – "Can you guess how I came to the conclusion summarized in this bullet?" "Can you guess what's coming next?"

Languages have sentences for a reason. They express complete thoughts. Presenters would be wise to work on short, concise, and *complete* sentences (with a subject, verb and object), rather than creating bullets that may ultimately do more to confuse than clarify.

What About Handouts?

The visuals that tell the business story are not limited to PowerPoint® slides. Printed materials exist – and for good reason.

There is no need to waste the real estate of a slide with an agenda – but an agenda can certainly be printed for each meeting participant. Likewise, a summary or extract of the key points of the presentation, along with a description of the approach and methodology, serves both the presenter and the audience better as a handout than as a slide. Handouts allow the presenter to concentrate on the story, and the handouts allow the audience to make notes and refer to the main points after the meeting. However – too many handouts can distract the audience from the presentation. A handout should cover the key points and no more – the focus is on *you*. You know the subject, and in the best situations, you know the audience. It is your decision as to when to distribute the handouts.

One further note: the best handouts are *not* usually reprints of the slides. A slide is designed to be visually exciting. It is also designed to be explained and expanded upon by the speaker. A handout is designed for reading and contemplation. It doesn't have to be limited by visual conventions. Think about what you want audience members to do with handouts and design them accordingly. If an audience member wants a copy of the presentation, then it can be sent after the meeting.

Get Help When You Can

As much as I love the personal computer, one of its unfortunate byproducts is that some people are convinced that everyone can be an accountant, writer, and graphic designer by mastering the Microsoft Office Suite. It hasn't worked out that way. While most of us have picked up a few pointers outside our disciplines, it still takes skilled professionals to create great output.

If you have access to graphic artists or to people with a flair for design, buy them gifts, tell them how great they look, and convince them to help you out whenever you can. That's what I do.

Entire books and websites are dedicated to graphic design and how we can all use type, color, and images to create effective meetings. I believe that the very first step after a draft of the story has been completed is to treat each slide like valuable territory. Create a site plan to get the most out of each slide, remembering the principles of *show, don't tell* and that *people think in ideas, not facts.*

Many of the design conventions that have supported business presentations have become outmoded as the definition of a "meeting" has changed (WebEx, teleconferencing, etc.), and people have become more pressed for time. The discipline of the **7-Slide Solution™** encourages presenters to make every slide count, and that means that wallpaper such as title slides and agendas have, at best, a limited role. Likewise, the notion that lots of white space is necessary for an idea to stand out may make sense on highway billboards, but it wastes space, and time, in a business setting.

Following the **7-Slide Solution™**, every presenter can develop his or her own design conventions to communicate ideas. This includes planting a question for the audience, evoking an emotion, giving the audience some food for thought, and then moving the story forward by answering the question.

7-Slide Solution™

Chapter 15
Slide 1: Engagement

I t's show time.

Now is the moment of truth when you put your best thinking on the line. The challenge is to transfer your ideas to the audience so that each member walks out with the same message. Your only goal now is to communicate concisely and compellingly.

To achieve your goal you must optimize every tool at your disposal. The storyline. The right facts. Your personal presentation style. And, of course, the 7 slides.

This chapter concentrates on the first slide of the presentation, where you, as the presenter, grab the attention of the audience and deliver an emotional impact.

Before the Meeting Starts, Create A Comfortable Environment

We live in a noisy, distracting environment. The people who attend your presentation may be shuffling from meeting to meeting in the course of a day. They have dozens of things on their minds. The meeting may be vital to you, but just one of a long series of meetings to them.

That's why it is so important to manage the time you have. This is par-

Create Dramatic Impact

1. Project a dark screen as the audience enters the room
2. Keep the conversation casual
3. Use handouts to set the stage

ticularly true of the time *before* the meeting begins. Typically, people don't arrive en masse for a meeting. They trickle in one at time. This is similar to the time spent in a theater waiting for a movie to begin. Audience members are eager for the film to begin, but also need some time to get comfortable, adjust to the lighting, and getting into the right frame of mind.

In a business or professional setting, you can use this time to create a dramatic climate for your presentation. The trick is to begin engaging the audience without engaging them too much.

Since slides are the main visual attraction, they should be held in reserve until the audience is settled and prepared. A dark screen (which can be achieved by projecting the first slide and pressing "b" on the keyboard), allows the audience to adjust from their previous meeting and start to think about the meeting at hand.

Simple, non-challenging handouts can also be used to warm up the audience and set the stage. Perhaps an article related to the subject, a précis or abstract of your presentation, or (if required) a printed agenda.

Whatever you decide, don't waste this valuable time. Create an environment that subtly plants the seeds of the message you are about to deliver.

Example 1: Demonstrate the Core Conflict

Novelists, moviemakers, journalists and other storytellers go to great lengths to create opening sentences and scenes that set up the storyline and grab the interest of the audience. The best way to accomplish this in a presentation is to use slide 1 to set up the core conflict.

Conflict naturally attracts us. Conflict creates that desire to "see what happens next..." Conflict sets the tone for the presentation because it:

> "In every presentation, begin with something familiar. Give your audience at least one fact they already know and tie that into the new material you are presenting. Give them something slightly familiar so they have a starting point, an initial connection to the new world you're bringing to them."
>
> *Richard Saul Wurman*
> *Information Anxiety 2*

1. Acknowledges to each audience member that you know the decision you are seeking may be difficult and that you will not waste time with simplistic analyses and solutions.

2. Frames the dimensions of the discussion. If you say the situation is about the need for "X" vs. the restraints of "Y," some in the audience may disagree but, in most cases, people will wait to see how the conflict plays out before raising too many objections.

3. Acts as both an agenda and objectives. The conflict combined with the natural desire to see how conflict is resolved creates a roadmap for the presentation. The audience will get it and follow along without intrusive reminders of "we are here" throughout the presentation.

4. Demonstrates that you have done your homework. It's almost impossible to develop a compelling conflict without accurate knowledge of the situation. Many presenters try to demonstrate this knowledge by spewing long lists of facts. A strong conflict slide accomplishes the same thing in a compact, compelling way.

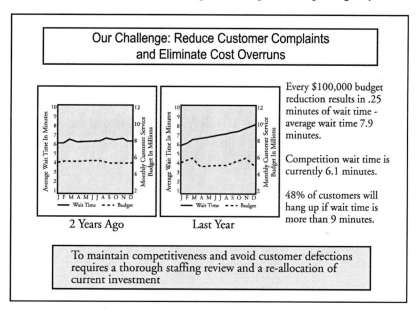

In this example, developed to resolve the problems facing the Customer Service team, the first slide is used to establish the core conflict. Audience attention is gained by planting the question: "How can we reduce customer complaints while eliminating the cost overruns?" This question is a challenge to the group and frames the presentation in the context of sustainability. Then, a partial answer is provided by demonstrating that the current approach is not working. This is accomplished by contrasting year-by-year performance in wait time along with budget allocations.

There are a few brief insights designed to evoke an emotional response (loss of competitiveness), as well as a peek into the future (if wait time increases, then there is a risk of losing a substantial number of customers). Notice that full sentences are used to express complete thoughts.

The slide moves the story forward by previewing a possible resolution – staff review and investment re-allocation.

In this single slide, the audience gains the following insights:

1. The current situation is more serious than the audience realized.
2. A factual analysis of the problem.
3. A look at the future – further wait time increases the risk for substantial customer defection.
4. An emotional jolt that some cognitive scientists believe will assist the audience in making a decision.

All in all, this is an opening that should satisfy most of the audience members.

Example 2: State Your Premise

Conflict is not the only way to generate interest. Some stories state the premise right up front and then proceed to prove (or disprove) it. The romantic comedy *When Harry Met Sally* states the premise early in the story when Harry matter-of-factly states: "Men and women can't be friends." The rest of the movie unfolds as a series of scenes to demonstrate how wrong he is. Non-fiction works – particularly political books or documentaries – often state the premise up front and successfully hold attention while they prove it.

Although I prefer to keep the premise in the background and let the audience discover it through the storyline, there may be situations when stating the premise at the start can be effective. Here are a few such situations:

1. *If the premise is so strong it's guaranteed to engage the audience.* If your work has uncovered a new theory or concept that will so rock conventional wisdom that it puts the attendees on the edges of their seats – by all means use it. Also, an informational presentation can announce the premise at the opening. For example, a meeting about a business re-organization where a presentation of the details will resolve the conflicts of apprehension and resistance in the audience.
2. *To challenge conventional wisdom.* You can choose a widely held premise and then *disprove* it.
3. *To distance yourself from the conclusions to come.* There may be times when you need some distance between yourself and the content of the presentation. This may be because you have become personally

associated with the premise to such an extent that it sounds like bias, or if the recommendations are so controversial that they are likely to cause arguments, then you might want to cite the premise by using an outside resource like "Research shows…" or "According to…"

4. *When the premise actually contains a conflict.* Some conflicts within your business or profession may be so recognizable (regulation, a powerful competitor or customer, etc.) that the mention of certain phrases may trigger the emotional response you are looking for. If that's the case, then consider stating your premise on the first slide.

The downside of stating your premise has two dimensions.

First, it removes most of the suspense. The audience knows what the story is about and is free to tune-out if their interest is not maintained.

Second, it sets up a potential conflict between presenter and audience. A premise is often an informed opinion. By stating the premise up front – without a lot of evidence or storyline – presenters may run into disagreements with certain audience members before they get started.

It's your choice. If you do decide to use the premise as your opening slide, then here are some thoughts on how to do it.

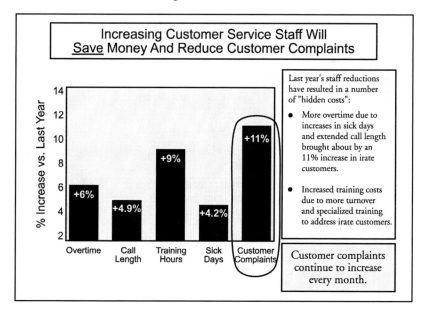

In this slide, the headline is the premise. The presenter offers strong conviction that the answer to the company's problems is to increase the staff of the Customer Service team.

Salient facts about hidden costs are provided and the alarming news of increases in customer complaints is highlighted.

By including sick days as a cost, the presenter shows that there may be human (burnout, stress) as well as financial costs.

The slide continues the momentum of the story by stating that complaints have continued to increase every month.

Many presentations that I have observed state the premise (after an avalanche of background data). I think your audience is smart enough to understand your premise without having to tell them. Most good stories leave it up to the listeners to draw the conclusions of the author. You should have the confidence to do the same.

Principles of Slide 1

Principles of Slide 1

1. Engage the audience emotionally and intellectually
2. Set the best tone
3. Turn browsers into an audience
4. Introduce the core conflict

Slide 1 of the **7-Slide Solution™** carries a heavy load. It must engage the audience, give people a sense of what's to come, and segue to the next slide.

You should have one and only one goal with the opening slide – to engage the audience. That means providing information to start a decision-making process while playing on emotions to create an environment where people are *motivated* to make the right decisions.

You control the tone of the dialogue that is about to take place. Do you want the environment to be feisty and a little argumentative? Or do you prefer a more relaxed, thoughtful climate? What you decide to do with the opening slide has a lot to do with the attitude people will adopt during the meeting.

Most of us attend so many meetings in the course of a year that we are like browsers in a bookstore. Just as most book purchasers make a decision to buy based on a quick read of the book jacket, we decide whether a meeting is relevant in the first few minutes. Recognizing this is central to becoming a successful persuader.

Finally, what interests people is conflict. So the core conflict should usually be part of the opening in every presentation you make.

Chapter 16
Slide 2: Backstory

A good presentation should be about what the presenter knows and what he or she wants other people to do about it. Perhaps it's a need to demonstrate how much work went into a presentation, or an attempt to gain credibility, but too many presenters want to explain *how* they came to know the conclusion and *why* their hard work should result in a favorable decision. They inundate the audience with background information about historical analyses, methodology, research hours, sources, and so on. The sad truth is: in most cases, *nobody cares.* Not only do they not care, in a way, too much background information gives the audience permission to tune out.

How many times have you been to a meeting and focused on other things until the presenter "got to the point?" Just as we don't need the entire life story of a movie character, we don't need to know the life story of a business idea or proposal.

Presenters are not alone in the struggle to determine how much background to provide. Even the most skilled storytellers contend with how much backstory to put in and how much to leave out.

This chapter examines the role of backstory in the business presentation and provides techniques for balancing the right amount of background with the need to keep the story moving forward.

Backstory

"Backstory is the set of significant events that occurred in the characters' past that the writer can use to build his story's progressions."

Robert McKee

One Story at a Time

Think of your favorite movie or novel. What you probably remember is the action. Stories describe what is going on in a specific period of time, and can quickly span years or decades because the writer determines the time frame. Characters don't just exist in a specific timeframe, however. They have pasts. The audience wants to know about what happened before the events they are witnessing. That's called backstory. Too little backstory makes the characters uninteresting. Too much forces us to make a choice as to what is more interesting – the present story or the backstory. That's a choice the audience of a business presentation shouldn't have to make. A successful presentation, like a good story, holds the right balance between the information being told and the backstory.

The best presentations unfold like a story in real time. What's happening in front of the audience – the visuals, the spoken words, and the transitions from point-to-point – is engaging and the best presenters know how to leverage it. It's a shame when presenters sacrifice that leverage to tell the audience another story of how they came to their insights and conclusions.

How Much Backstory Is Enough?

To achieve that delicate balance between too much and too little backstory, here are a few questions that, when answered, should help you decide:

1. If I were this audience, what (if anything) would I want to know about the work that went into the presentation?
2. What background information is *absolutely necessary* to make the presentation understandable?
3. What background information adds to the audience's interest to see what happens next?
4. Am I adding information in order to show how hard I worked to reach this resolution? If yes, will anyone care?

"How much backstory is enough?": whatever amount makes the presentation understandable and emotionally satisfying to the audience. *Not a word more.*

Why Use Slide 2 for Backstory?

Slide 2 is often the best scene to tell the backstory for at least four reasons.

First, slide 1 is designed to engage the audience. Whether you revealed the core conflict or stated your premise – there is an emotional impact from slide 1. You have taken a stand. People will naturally ask, "How did she reach that insight?" Slide 2 is not a bad place to step back and spend a few minutes describing how you got to this point.

110

Second, using slide 2 for backstory allows the audience to digest slide 1. By bringing in backstory at this point, the presenter is saying, "You have my permission to mull over what I discussed in slide 1 while I review some history."

Third, if your backstory has an interesting twist, then it can enhance your credibility. For example, if you used an innovative methodology or sourced a unique database, then explaining that may further engage the audience – "She knows her stuff."

Use Slide 2 for Backstory

1. Describe how you arrived at this point
2. Allow the audience to consider slide 1
3. Enhance your credibility
4. Build a bridge to the tension of the story

Finally, positioning the backstory here can be an effective bridge between the engagement role of slide 1 and the tension-building role of slide 3. The logic flow is: "I told you the problem (slide 1), here's how I came to that conclusion (slide 2), and here's what will happen if we don't do something about it (slide 3)."

There's no rule that says you *must* use slide 2 for backstory. If you think the presentation will have more impact by using slide 3 or 4 or 5 for backstory, then that is where the backstory scene should be positioned in the story.

My advice is *not* to use slide 1 for backstory. Why? The audience may become confused. Is this a presentation about how a problem was researched and analyzed? Or is it a presentation about a problem and how to solve it?

If your audience is extremely familiar with the topic of your presentation, and is fully aware of the history of the current situation, then the backstory may not be necessary. In that case, you can eliminate slide 2 and move your story toward the tension scenes.

The One and Only Backstory Question

The backstory slide should follow the same pattern as any other scene. You will want to plant a question in the minds of the audience members, evoke an emotion, answer the question, and point to the next scene.

Whether in a story or a presentation, there is only one backstory question –

How to Develop a Successful Scene

1. Plant a question
2. Evoke a specific emotion
3. Answer the question
4. Move the story forward

"How did he or she get here?" If you are successful in engaging the audience in slide 1, there is the tendency to ask, "Is this a casual observation or did some real work go into this? How did she get here?"

Answering that question with enough emotional impact is the secret of a successful backstory slide.

Example 1: Source Review

For a presenter, using a backstory slide means getting in and out quickly. To share just enough information to satisfy the curiosity of the audience and bridge to the next slide.

This example provides only the sources of information that were used to build the presentation about Customer Service department problems...

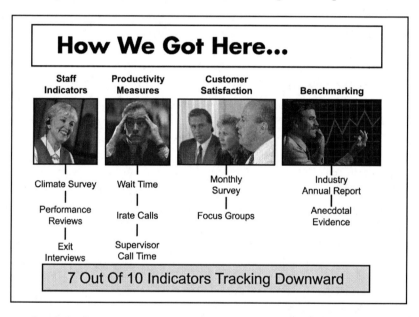

The slide demonstrates the breadth of the effort but avoids too much detail about the methodology or the data that came out of the effort. The headline asks the one and only backstory question directly. The fact that 7 out of 10 indicators are tracking downward provides the emotional impact.

A slide like this might be satisfactory for an audience that is not technically savvy in your function. It is specific enough to provide comfort that due diligence was performed without being overwhelmingly so. An audience more steeped in the day-to-day workings of your function, however, would probably find this unsatisfying and will want to know about the protocols followed and at least some of the data uncovered.

Example 2: Methodology and Key Data

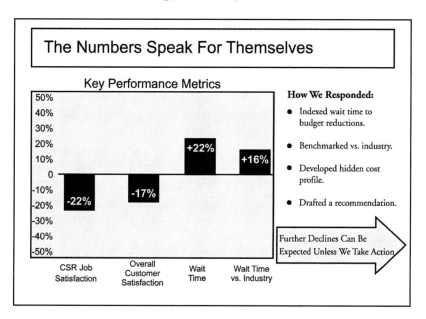

This slide combines key data along with a review of what the presenter did in response to the data. The headline camouflages the backstory role of the slide but raises the backstory question none the less. The emotional impact is realized by the graph, which shows relatively poor performance in the key metrics, as well as by the tag line: "Further declines can be expected..." Although the message is in the graph, the bullet points help the audience to understand the approach taken.

This type of slide would be more satisfactory to audience members who are familiar with the function. No matter what the audience's degree of familiarity, it is critical that the presenter has all of the supporting data in the event that numbers or conclusions are challenged.

Principles of Slide 2

The backstory scene of the **7-Slide Solution™** should only be used when necessary to satisfy the demands of your audience. The key to a successful backstory scene is to get in and out quickly. This slide is a device to give your story context, but not a story in itself.

Principles of Slide 2

1. If not needed, don't include the backstory
2. Don't tell another story
3. Don't get bogged down
4. Know your audience

If you do use a backstory, then make sure that it does not become another presentation within your presentation. You do not want to provide so much historical evaluation that it distracts from the core conflict – you do not want to give so much data analysis that the audience tunes out and loses sight of your premise.

This relates directly to the next principle – don't become so involved with the backstory that the present story is stopped in its tracks. Presenting details about research protocols naturally invites questions and comments, and these discussions can derail the entire presentation.

The use of backstory and how to control it is determined by your knowledge of the audience. If the participants are familiar with the issues, then omit the backstory. If a general background and update is required to make everyone comfortable, then provide that information and no more. If your group members demand to know how you developed certain conclusions, then tell them and move on.

From the backstory, you must return to the main storyline by creating the interest to see what happens as a result of this background. To make the transition as seamless as possible, include a tag line on the backstory slide to move your story – and your audience – forward.

The bottom line? Do your best to avoid getting bogged-down with a lot of backstory. It will do more to kill a good presentation than bad visuals, poor structure, or even a nervous presenter.

Chapter 17
Slide 3: Build Tension

The opening slide of the **7-Slide Solution™** is designed to engage your audience, usually by demonstrating the core conflict – either directly or indirectly.

Based on your knowledge of the audience, you may have used the second slide to provide some history and an explanation of how you arrived at your resolution.

Now you are ready to build a dramatic impact by creating the sense of urgency that is needed to make decisions. This chapter gives you advice on building tension in the business story, and provides principles that can be applied every time.

It's All About Consequences

Tension is the energy within a story that compels the listeners to see what happens next. A good story establishes a core conflict for the main characters and then describes how the characters *decide* to handle it. In essence, a good story is no more than an examination of what characters do or don't do to resolve conflicts. A good business presentation is a similar examination.

How to Develop a Successful Scene

1. Plant a question
2. Evoke a specific emotion
3. Answer the question
4. Move the story forward

Any conflict – from the simplest to the most complex – is a series of questions that must be examined in order to move toward a resolution. Suppose you are trying to decide between a romantic vacation with your spouse or a trip to Disney World with your kids. Simply stated, the core conflict is romance vs. family fun. As you mull over this decision, you begin to ask yourself some questions.

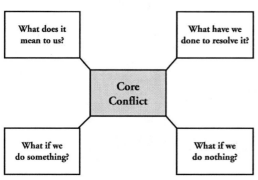

EXPLORING CONSEQUENCES

What does it mean to us?

What have we done to resolve it?

Core Conflict

What if we do something?

What if we do nothing?

The first question is something like, *What does resolving this really mean to us?* You and your spouse may truly need to get away – alone. On the other hand, nothing can match the fun of a family vacation and watching the kids have a good time. There are consequences – favorable and unfavorable – no matter which way you go.

The second question is – *What have we done to resolve this conflict so far?* Have you and you spouse discussed the subject seriously? Have you evaluated the costs, both monetary and emotional?

The third question may not be in the forefront, but it is certainly in the background somewhere – *Suppose we do nothing?* See if the kids or your spouse bring it up. At least you don't have to think about it for a while.

The final question you might ask yourself is – *What if we do something?* Even if it's just order some brochures or check airfares.

All decisions – the important diplomatic decisions that affect global stability or the smaller decisions about what to eat for lunch – are made in much the same way. That provides presenters with an excellent opportunity to build tension.

The progression of questions evokes an emotional response. What does it mean to us? – *gain or loss.* What have we done to resolve it? – *confidence or regret.* What if we do nothing? – possible *risk.* What if we do something? – possible *reward.* You can almost feel the emotional temperature rising as one question builds upon another. This is especially true if there are no easy answers to the questions.

That is the goal of slide 3: to increase resonance by exploring the consequences of resolving or *not* resolving the core conflict.

Let the Tension Mount

As you prepare the tension scenes of your presentation, think about all the consequences of *not* resolving the core conflict. Then, organize the consequences in ascending emotional order – from the least emotionally resonant consequences to the most emotional.

Then, think about the consequences of resolving the core conflict and organize them in ascending emotional order.

In general, potential loss resonates more powerfully than potential gain. So the consequences of *not* resolving the core conflict will usually create more tension.

When you design slide 3, start with the least emotional issues and build to the most resonant. In the Customer Service example, the presenter may have identified staff morale, operational, and competitive consequences if the core conflict is not resolved. The presenter may also have identified better staff morale, and a more positive environment for future contract negotiations as positive consequences of resolving the core conflict. They may rate the financial consequences of the conflict as having the least resonance and explore that issue first, then operational, and so on. In fact, they may reserve the *most* resonant consequence for slide 4 – *bring it to a boil.*

When ranking these consequences, evaluate them from the *audience's* perspective, not yours.

Example 1: Insistence vs. Resistance

One way to build tension is to demonstrate what has already been done and the results of those actions. Novelist James Frey calls this "insistence vs. resistance."

In effect, this approach builds tension by showing that many actions have been tried, but each has been met with an equal counter-action.

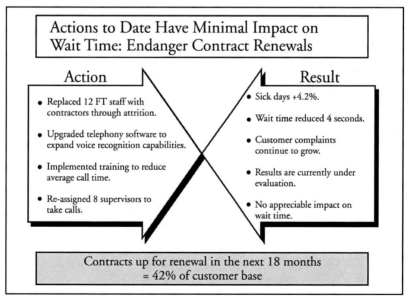

In this slide, the presenter plants a question – "What has been done to address the core conflict?" – and evokes emotions by reviewing the potential loss of contracts if service does not improve.

The question is answered with a detailed list of actions and the results of each action. The tension is built by going point-by-point and seeing, in this case, how little has been accomplished.

The line at the bottom introduces the "keystone data point" and previews the next scene that will provide more detail about the potential contract losses.

You should only use this approach if two conditions are met. First, you must be confident that you have tried many options and executed well (this can be demonstrated with the backstory slide). Second, you must have at least one more option up your sleeve that will be revealed in the resolution.

Example 2: The Problem is Bigger Than You Think

Most people don't really seek the optimum solution to a problem – they find the most acceptable solution and then stop thinking about it. They *satisfice*.

That's fine if you don't want your audience to think too much. However, if your proposal requires deeper thought, then you will want to expand the problem beyond the core conflict.

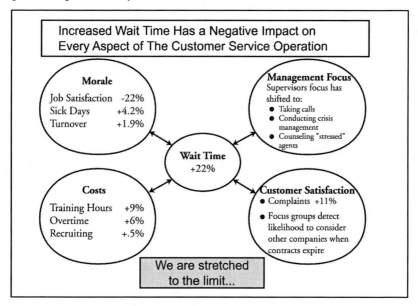

In this example, the question is posed – "What is the real impact?" An emotional element is introduced in the title with the words, "Negative impact on every aspect…"

Graphically, the wait time issue is positioned as the causal center of a host of qualitative and quantitative business problems. Because this slide will be projected for a few minutes, the presenter will have the time to direct the audience through the slide and explain all of the points listed.

The scene provides an emotional impact with an urgent plea for help.

This approach is best used when you have solid facts to back up the claims. It is also effective when quantitative and qualitative issues are combined, such as including anecdotal observations like stress levels or employee morale with statistical evidence of performance.

Example 3: The "Drill Down"

Another way to build tension is to look more closely at a fact presented earlier.

This can be accomplished by investigating the data and expanding the urgency so that the threat or benefit is greater than it initially appears.

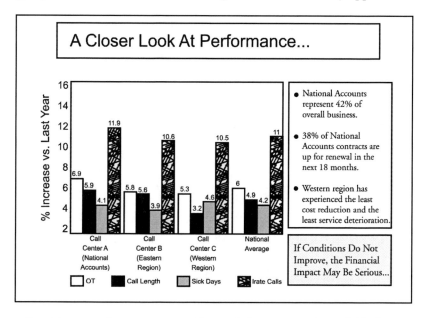

In this example, company-wide statistics are used to drill down to regional and national account data to drive home the point that the situation is deteriorating – especially in the most important business segment, national accounts.

Emotion is added by reminding the audience that contracts are up for renewal and may be at risk.

The slide includes a pointer to the next scene previewing possible negative financial impacts – "If conditions do not improve…"

This approach is particularly effective if your data is very thorough and you can draw a credible conclusion. The danger for some presenters is going too deep on this drill down. The temptation of falling in love with your data is always there. It takes discipline to avoid investigating so deeply that you distract the audience and re-direct their focus to backstory.

Principles of Slide 3

Principles of Slide 3

1. Return the audience from the backstory to the main story
2. Explore the consequences of resolving and *not* resolving the core conflict
3. Present the consequences in order of emotional impact
4. Create a sense of urgency

Slide 3 creates tension and moves the audience toward the decision.

If you provided a backstory in slide 2, then your first job is to bring the audience back to your main storyline. This may not be as simple as it sounds. Some audience members may be more interested in your backstory than your main story.

In most cases, the core conflict is communicated in slide 1 – engagement. Slide 3 is designed to stretch that core conflict and to build resonance by exploring the consequences of resolving and *not* resolving the core conflict.

Slide 3 is a pivotal slide. Slide 1 gets the audience thinking. If used for backstory, slide 2 provides the rationale and may enhance the presenter's credibility. Slide 3 is where the audience is moved from just considering an idea to starting to think about taking action on it.

One of the best ways to execute that pivot is to create an emotional continuum: presenting the least emotional issues first and then allowing the tension to mount by presenting more emotionally jarring points as you proceed through the slide.

The overall goal is to create an intense sense of urgency and, as with the other slides, the need to see what happens next…

Chapter 18
Slide 4: Bring It To A Boil

By this stage of a successful presentation, you have created interest through conflict and tension. The audience wants to see what happens next.

This chapter shows you how to bring "pressure" to the story so that the audience is looking for a release from the tension and is searching for a resolution. The chapter provides the principles that create that desire for release and position you, as the presenter, as the person the audience seeks to provide it.

Bring Pressure to Bear

Slide 4 brings your presentation – and the audience – to the brink. It creates enough additional tension so that people are a bit anxious, but not so much that they just give up. Developing the right amount of tension is a challenge for every presenter or storyteller.

There are two goals for slide 4. First, bring the tension to a head. Second, help the audience make the transition from thinking about a problem to doing something about it.

It seems that many presentations are won or lost at this point. Proposals are won if the presenter can weave in enough consternation and concern that the audience looks to him or her for an answer. Proposals are lost if the presenter indiscriminately piles worry and stress on the tension points that he or she has created in slide 3. There is a risk here – we have a limited tolerance for stress and most people will look for an escape, which may mean that they simply tune out.

For these reasons, I believe that it is well worth your time to put some extra thought and effort into the design of slide 4.

The Do's and Don't's of Creating Pressure

- Do reinforce the urgency of the situation – Don't repeat what has already been stated
- Do evoke emotions – Don't be melodramatic
- Do save the most dramatic points for last – Don't stretch it so far that the audience snaps
- Do bring the story to a head – Don't provide resolution, yet
- Do remind the audience what's at stake – Don't preach

There are a few do's and don't's to follow when preparing "boiling point" scenes.

Slide 4 should *reinforce* the urgency that was provided in the previous slides. That's reinforce, *not* repeat. The urgency can be heightened by expanding on it. For example, if slide 3 showed an opportunity to save money, then use slide 4 to show how that money could be spent more productively. If a problem with productivity was examined in slide 3, then use slide 4 to show how that problem could lead to a loss of competitiveness.

In the ideal presentation, slide 4 resonates with emotion. By reinforcing the sense of urgency, emotional pressure is applied and the audience will look for a way to find relief. But if the presenter goes too far, it becomes melodrama. Dire warnings and gloomy predictions undermine the presenter's credibility and diminish interest in what he or she is saying.

Slide 4 is where you should locate your most powerful idea along with the most powerful facts to support it. It is the key slide for moving from consideration to action. Avoid the use of "reveals" (building a slide bullet-by-bullet): the audience already senses the urgency and does not need mind games. Fight the urge to over explain: if the story has been well developed, then people will get it. If it hasn't been well developed, then a lengthy explanation of why a particular fact is important isn't likely to bring them on board. Project the slide, say what you need to say, and let the slide stand while the audience ponders it.

When the audience looks to you for an answer, you may be tempted to give one. Try to suppress the urge. There's a step between bringing the story to a boil and providing resolution – the turning point (which is reviewed in the next chapter).

Slide 4 is where you provide strong motivation to act. Steer clear of the tendency to preach. This goes back to the concept of "show, don't tell." If you have said the right words and projected the right images, then there's no need for you to take to the soapbox.

Example 1: The Summary of Consequences

Cognitive scientists have demonstrated the limitations of short-term memory. If you spent time on slide 3 detailing some of the consequences of not resolving the core conflict, then there is a good chance that some audience members could use a reminder.

One way to provide that reminder as well as bring the tension to a boil is to use a summary of consequences. This approach brings all the consequences communicated in slide 3 and reformats the message to add another dollop of emotion.

Returning to the Customer Service example, the presenter begins the summary in the headline: "Budget cuts = Service declines." Fifteen seconds per call is then translated into an hourly and daily figure based on typical call volume. Keeping customers waiting for nearly 21 hours a day resonates a lot more than 15 seconds per call.

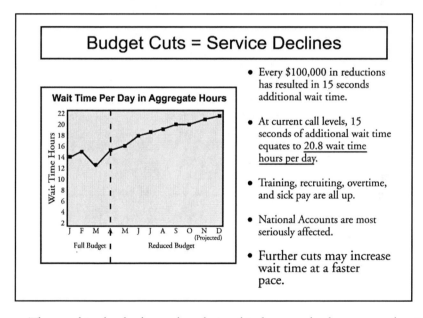

The graphic clearly shows the relationship between budget cuts and wait time. The cuts took place in April and the wait time went in the opposite direction. The final bullet point – that additional budget cuts will result in an even greater loss of service – sets the stage for my next slide.

This approach is most successful when you feel you have made a strong case in the first 3 slides and want to hammer home the message you have already delivered.

Example 2: The "Killer" Statistic

Another way to bring the tension to a boil is to hold the most dramatic fact or statistic in reserve until you arrive at slide 4. This can focus the audience on the true dimensions of the possible gain or loss.

A word of caution about using the "killer" statistic: just because you think it's overwhelming doesn't mean the audience will. Remember that you are intimately involved with the data related to your function. Others are not. You can attach all kinds of meanings to a statistic that a "civilian" cannot. Test the "killer statistic" with people both within and outside your function. If they think it's a killer – then use it. If they don't, then bring things to a boil with a different technique.

Declining Service Levels Jeopardize Contract Renewals

Value of Total Renewals In The Next 18 Months

$300 Million

- Irate calls are up 11% among near term renewal customers.

- 6% of customers surveyed indicate they will seek additional "inconvenience discounts."

- Competitors are actively marketing their service advantages in trade publications.

Management "Tweaks" Are No Longer Enough

In this slide the potential for lost revenue is highlighted – $300 million. This puts the problem into the perspective of sustainability that everyone in the audience can understand.

The statistics listed on the right side serve to underscore the risk. Customers are angry. They are looking for compensation and the competitors are at the door.

The tension is further heightened by the comment "Management tweaks are no longer enough." This begs the question – "What is enough?" – which sets up slide 5.

This approach is most effective when you have a powerful fact that will hold the audience's attention. It can also be used if you had to include several statistics earlier in the presentation. If there is one data point that truly sums up all the others, then you can use the killer statistic to great effect.

Example 3: No Escape – Or Is There?

Think of how many movies you've seen where the main character seems to run through every option and fails to achieve his goal. Then, just at the last moment, an opportunity presents itself and the character is able to move forward. *Apollo 13, The Fugitive, Indiana Jones,* and hundreds of popular movies follow this pattern.

A similar technique can be used in business presentations. It involves showing how conventional options have been exhausted, then springing a resolution later in the presentation.

Management Options Are Dwindling – Competitors Are Aggressive

Wait Time +22%, Despite:

- Supervisor Reassignments
- Software Upgrades
- Specialized Training
- Efficiency Bonuses
- Shift Realignments
- Temp Hirings

Competitive Ad in Trade Journal

For this slide, the presenter communicates the feeling of no escape in the headline. Options are dwindling and the enemy is approaching. This creates a sense of urgency that the audience can relate to.

The graphic of the competitor's ad is a powerful image that demonstrates how real the threat is.

The simple list of the actions taken to date offers powerful evidence that the headline is not just a scare tactic. All the standard management responses – compensation, staffing, outsourcing, training, staffing – have been tried. Still wait time grows. What to do?

It takes courage to use this approach. Few managers want to admit that they are out of ideas – even momentarily. However this may be the best approach for bringing things to a boil and launching the audience into decision making mode because it causes discomfort. If you, the expert, have tried everything, what is left? That is exactly the kind of discomfort that slide 4 is designed to evoke.

Principles of Slide 4

Principles of Slide 4

1. Raise the tension – but not too much

2. Create more emotional resonance than any other slide

3. Suppress the urge to provide resolution

Slide 4 may be the trickiest scene in the 7-**Slide Solution**™, but it is rewarding when done well. It's risky because if you turn the tension too high, then the audience will shut down and you may be perceived as the "boy who cried wolf." Rewarding because if you get the tension right, the rest of the presentation and the decision are smooth sailing.

This is the point in the presentation where you want emotions to run high. You want the participants to be uncomfortable. If they were complacent they should now be concerned. If they felt confident they should now be a little shaky. Work the audience to the point where the tension is almost unbearable.

Whatever you do, don't offer resolution. Not yet. Offering resolution at this point can appear manipulative. There's another step to take before you're ready to offer relief.

Slide 4 is the scene of the presentation where you invest the most of yourself. You may show some vulnerability if, for example, you communicate solutions you tried that failed to get the desired results. You may share some numbers that you would rather senior managers not see. On the other hand, this scene can set you (the presenter) as the "hero." You control the flow of information from problem to solution. If you have created enough resonance through slide 4, the audience is primed to listen to your resolution.

Now that the audience needs to relieve the tension and urgency, it's time to cool things down. You are at the turning point.

Chapter 19
Slide 5: Offer Choice(s)

Slide 5 is where you relieve the tension that you have developed throughout the presentation and provide a glimpse of a better way. It is also the place where you confront the audience with the need to make a decision.

The turning point of a compelling business story should:

1. Relieve the tension.
2. Offer a choice.
3. Examine the consequences of action or inaction.

This chapter gives guidelines on framing the decision by limiting the choices for the audience.

Frame the Decision

Good storytellers recognize that there is only one way out of tense situations: someone must make a decision. The same is true of a business presentation. After delivering information about problems or opportunities, considering implications and adding the emotional impact of the boiling point slide, there is only one way out: *somebody has to make a decision.*

Unlike a storyteller, a business presenter does not have total control. The storyteller can dictate what he or she wants the character to do based on the actions the author unfolds in previous scenes. A presenter can't do that. The story must be turned over to the audience participants so that *they* can make the decision.

The writers of the U.S. Constitution are often called the Framers. They realized that the document they were creating was not the final word on how the country should always be governed. They framed the core beliefs and principles but also provided the mechanisms for future generations to add to these principles through amendments.

That's what scene 5 should accomplish. By framing the decision that *you* want the audience to make, people can think about the resolution within a structure that *you* establish. Typical business problems and opportunities can have any number of possible solutions. In some cases, you may want to explore those possibilities through brainstorming or other techniques. N*ot* in a business presentation. Slide 5 is used to influence, as much as possible, how the members of the audience *think* about resolving the conflict you have put before them.

Limit the Choices

One way to influence the audience's thinking and effectively frame a decision is to limit the number of choices.

While good consensus building suggests that you offer many possibilities, good communication does not. Picture an action film where the hero must choose between saving the world or saving his family. Saving the world or saving his friends. Finding inner peace or preventing future wars. Too many choices can dilute the tension by forcing the listeners to decide which option they want to focus on. It may also reduce their ability to actually make a decision by overloading short-term memory.

What is the optimal number of choices you should offer in a business presentation? In most cases...*one.*

The best business stories offer a simple choice between:

1. Maintaining the status quo – not changing and trying to overcome the known consequences, and...
2. Changing the current situation – facing different and unknown consequences.

Not every complex decision can be broken down into such a specific choice. Many can.

Example 1: The Fork in the Road

Slide 5 can be called the moment of truth, the climax, the turning point, or the fork in the road. The objective is to frame the decision in a way that influences the audience to think about resolution in your terms.

One approach is to present the task before the audience as an "either/or" proposition. Either we act or we don't. Either we tackle a problem or we don't. Either we lead, follow, or get out of the way.

In this slide, the title poses the question, "What do we do next?" It evokes emotions of fear by focusing the audience on the unknown future.

The two choices – status quo or change – are visually represented so that the audience can compare the relative attractiveness of each.

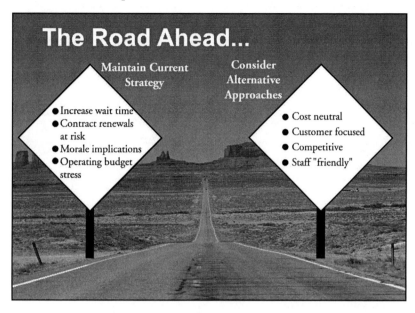

The question is answered by listing some of the consequences of maintaining the status quo and some of the challenges of implementing change.

This slide moves the story forward by using the word "consider." This implies that if you ask me to consider something, then you will tell me what it is you want me to consider. In this case, that means resolution.

This slide does not offer any details about the *plan* for change. That's because I am using slide 5 to frame the decision, not offer resolution. Too much detail at this point will cloud the issue and will lead to discussion about the best way to execute instead of deciding which way to go.

Example 2: Multiple-Choice

Although I always look for an either/or choice, I recognize, because of complexity or corporate culture, that it is not always possible to do so.

In those situations, a method of framing the choice is to examine a series of options and their possible consequences in a multiple-choice layout.

One advantage to framing the decision using this method is that you can make certain choices relatively unattractive in comparison to the choices you want the audience to make.

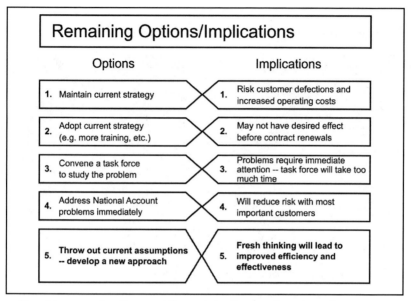

For this example, the word "remaining" is used in the title. It resonates with the audience as "Time is running out, we don't have many options left." The headline also plants the question, "What can we do?"

The question is answered by offering five options. The "wrong" choices are presented in order of unattractiveness: staying the course first and the National Account issue last. The slide biases the communication by showing the preferred choice in slightly larger and bolder type. Color could also be used to set this choice apart from the others.

The final implication continues the story by using the term "Fresh thinking..." in anticipation that the audience will be interested in hearing about these new thoughts and will stay tuned for the next slide.

This is not my preferred way of creating the turning point. It disrupts the story line by forcing the audience to consider each option separately. However if you decide you cannot reduce the decision to an either/or proposition, then this may be appropriate.

Example 3: The Emotional Appeal

Emotions are important contributors to the decision-making process, and every slide should be designed to evoke some emotions in the audience.

A third way to frame the turning point of the presentation is to appeal directly to the emotions: "Do the right thing," "Show some guts," "Demonstrate pride in what we are doing." This approach can create a more receptive environment for change.

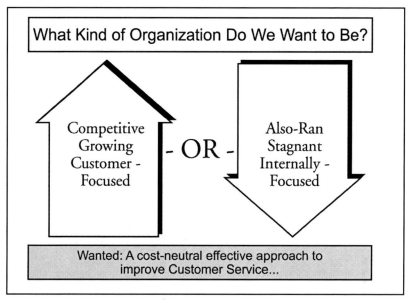

In this slide, the question is planted in the title – "What kind of organization do we want to be?" This question evokes emotions of pride in the audience (and perhaps some guilt that the group is not measuring up to its ideals).

The "either/or" proposition is presented in emotional terms.

The next scene is hinted at the bottom by promising a cost-neutral, effective solution.

Using emotion in designing slide 5 works if you have the personal credibility and stature to make such a challenge. For example, if you are perceived to have made substantial contributions over time, then you can pull off an emotional appeal. However, this can be a risky approach if you don't have such stature: it could be perceived as presumptuous.

Principles of Slide 5

Slide 5 is about influencing the way people think about decisions. It is not about the decision itself.

It is an important scene in the presentation because it tests whether or not you have proven the premise of your story. If the audience accepts the choices you present, then it's an indicator that people accept what you have been

Principles of Slide 5

1. Frame the decision to *your* advantage
2. Offer one choice – status quo or change
3. Don't offer resolution
4. Appeal to the emotions

presenting. If they resist and raise objections, then it means that the story is not complete for them.

Unlike a story, where the author controls the decisions the characters make, a presentation asks the *audience* to make the decision. The presenter cedes control at a critical point in the story flow. That doesn't mean he or she loses all influence, however. Slide 5 is where the presenter shapes the way the audience thinks about the conflict and ultimate resolution by framing the decision to favor his or her view.

The best way to turn the story over to the audience and to frame a decision is to offer a simple either/or proposition. In effect, this gives the audience *one* choice to consider – the status quo or a change.

Despite the strong temptation to offer a way out of the dilemma, use slide 5 to set up the resolution, *not* actually provide it.

Decisions are about emotions as well as intellect. Don't be reluctant to use both to maximum effect.

Chapter 20
Slide 6: Provide Resolution

You made an intellectual and emotional case. You provided a view of how you came to your insights. You examined consequences. You offered a choice.

The time has come to resolve the conflict and tension you created in the earlier scenes.

This chapter presents a single rule to follow in constructing the resolution scene of the story, and then discusses how to develop a successful resolution.

One Hard and Fast Rule for the Resolution Slide

There are limitless ways to create and present the slides in the **7-Slide Solution™**. You can change the order. You can state the premise or not. You can *show* the core conflict or *tell* the core conflict. No matter how you structure the story, one rule you *must* follow is – resolve the core conflict.

Conflict is the engine that drives the story. Conflict stimulates the interest and the emotional response. The conflict is the major contributor to the desire to see what happens next… If you fail to resolve the conflict, you will face dissatisfied, maybe even angry, audience members – audience members who will not be inclined to make the decisions you want them to make.

Two Ways to Resolve Most Conflicts

1. Designate one side as the winner.

2. Find a way to achieve the objectives of both sides without destroying either side.

In general, a conflict exists when two more-or-less equally strong forces oppose each other as each tries to attain an objective. Most conflicts are resolved either by declaring one of the forces as the winner *or* by demonstrating a way that both forces can achieve what they want without destroying each other. A movie like *Jaws* picks a winner (man) and a loser (shark). In a story like the *Wizard of Oz,* each character achieves what he or she wants in unexpected ways. These are satisfying endings to a business presentation as well.

Of the two ways to resolve a business conflict, the most attractive and satisfying is the second – find a way to achieve the objectives of both sides of the argument without destroying either side. These are variously known as win/win, mediated, or "have your cake and eat it, too" resolutions. They are satisfying because there are no losers.

As world affairs and basic human existence demonstrate, these resolutions are also the most difficult to develop. Sometimes we just have to pick a winner.

Focus on "What," Let Them *Ask* "How"

Many presenters who communicate their ideas effectively often destroy their good work by offering a plodding, overly-detailed resolution. Once again, the perceived need to demonstrate thorough preparation overwhelms the storyline and lessens the impact.

How to Develop a Successful Scene

1. Plant a question
2. Evoke a specific emotion
3. Answer the question
4. Move the story forward

The resolution slide is a way to show *what* must be done to resolve the core conflict and what can happen as a result of that resolution. This scene is not a description of an action plan. The goal is not to engage in a debate about the details.

My advice is to focus – clearly and entirely – on your proposal. Create a powerful *top line* message that communicates your strategic grasp of how to resolve the conflict. Let the audience ask *how* you intend to execute the plan.

Obviously, you must be prepared with as much detail as required to persuade your audience effectively. The *how* can be another story – the sequel to this story – which you can launch when this story is finished.

Slide 6 of the presentation must keep the momentum of the story going. Audience requests regarding how you intend to make things happen is one of the best indicators that people want to see what happens next...

Example 1: Mirror the Engagement Slide

If there is one thing about stories that most people dislike it is loose ends. We don't want to leave a theater asking, "What happened to character A?" or "The director never showed how situation X worked out." We demand the satisfaction of knowing how things turned out in every aspect of the story.

The same is true of a business presentation. One easy way to ensure that you satisfy this audience need is to mirror the engagement scene (usually the first slide). The engagement slide normally depicts the core conflict. The resolution slide is simply the response to the questions, challenges, or claims made in slide 1. You can even mirror the graphic look and colors of slide 1 to drive home the point that you are closing the loop.

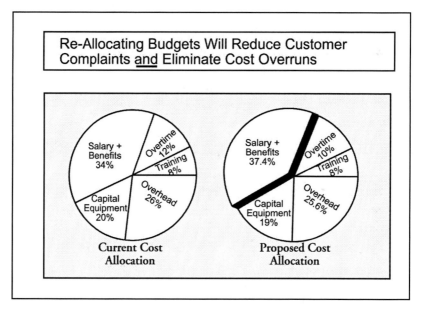

This example mirrors the core conflict of reducing customer complaints while maintaining budget limits. The key word in the headline is "and." The proposal is to reduce complaints *and* eliminate cost overruns. Classic "have your cake and eat it, too" resolutions are always expressed with "and." Selecting a winner, of course, is more one-sided.

The graphic shows how a budget re-alignment will allow sufficient staffing to reduce wait times while maintaining the current budget levels.

However a sacrifice is required. Staffing costs will recur (fixed) as long as people are employed, while the areas for reduction (capital investment and overhead) are variable. The presenter could include a lengthy explanation of how normal turnover rates allow for staff reductions by attrition and other details, but why break the flow? The audience knows that the plan is to resolve the issue by budget re-alignment, and will *conceptually* accept or reject that resolution. Asking how the conflict between fixed vs. variable costs will be resolved is another story and another opportunity to keep the audience wanting to see what happens next...

Example 2: "Happily Ever After"

In a well-told story, listeners want to know what decisions characters make at the "moment of truth." They also want to know how that decision affected the characters' lives. That is the final scene when all the loose ends are tied up and we get a sense of how the decision is working (or not working) out for the characters.

A business presentation has much the same dynamic. The presenter has made the case and offered a way forward. The audience participants want to see how that way forward will affect them and the business. The difference is, unlike a story, the decision has not yet been made. The presenter must *forecast or project* the likely outcome (not a guarantee) of accepting his or her advice.

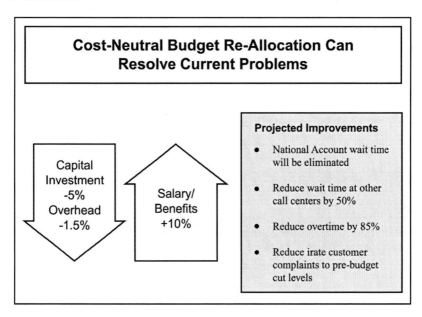

In this slide, some of the tension is relieved with the words "cost neutral" in the title. This eases the minds of those audience members who are budget conscious. "Resolve current problems" eases the tensions for everyone.

The re-alignment strategy is demonstrated in a simple graphic that shows what the presenter proposes.

The entire right side of the slide details the "happily ever after" implications of accepting the proposal.

Will the audience ask "how?" Is that a bad thing? Absolutely not. Asking "how" is just another indicator that the audience wants to see what happens next...

Example 3: Q&A

A good story raises a lot of questions and, for reasons of dramatic impact, doesn't always answer them right away.

Sometimes it's not a bad idea to remind the audience of the questions raised. Then answer them.

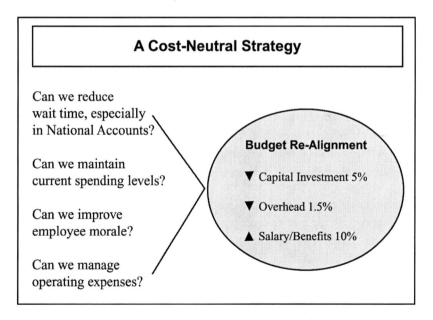

This slide uses the headline to answer the question, "Can we find a cost-neutral way to solve these problems?" It also plants another question: "How?"

This slide reminds the audience of both the emotional and intellectual issues that were raised during the story by listing a series of powerful questions. It answers all the questions with a straightforward resolution that is summarized by three actions of budget re-alignment.

If you choose to use a slide like this, I recommend that you show it, not tell it. It is so simple that is bound to raise questions of "how" – and that is exactly what you are seeking.

Principles of Slide 6

Principles of Slide 6

1. Resolve the core conflict
2. Answer questions the story raised
3. Focus on "what," let them *ask* "how"
4. Show, don't tell

The resolution slide may be the most satisfying from the presenter's viewpoint. If successfully executed, slide 6 calms the emotions, demonstrates the presenter's best thinking, and continues to engage the audience by encouraging people to ask, "how?"

A well-executed slide 6 achieves all this by first and foremost resolving the core conflict that started the story. The story platform takes that core conflict and stretches it, examines it from multiple angles, instills it with emotional resonance and finally says, "here's how to resolve it." A very satisfying experience.

Resolving conflict means answering the questions that you raised during the presentation. Don't leave the audience hanging with an unanswered question. It irritates people and can really diminish the chances for a decision that reflects your way of thinking.

The worst thing any presenter can do with the resolution scene is bog it down with details. This is not the place for action plans and time charts and assignment of responsibilities. This is the place to put your best *strategic* thinking on display and encourage the audience to ask for the details.

The advice to "show, don't tell" is especially applicable to slide 6. You want to generate questions. You want to have the audience asking for more. Design slide 6 so that it is logical, dramatic, and reflects your best thinking. Then, explain it minimally and stand back and let the audience react.

Premise, core conflict, tension, turning point and resolution – that's the end of the story, right?

Not quite. While your story may be solid, it's unlikely that it answered *every* question of *every* audience member. That's the job of slide 7.

Chapter 21
Slide 7: Set Up The Sequel

A good story leaves us wanting more. If we have been engaged enough to care what happens next, that interest doesn't end when the credits roll or we close the book. We want to hear more. Hollywood recognizes this. As of 2005, there have been twenty *James Bond* movies, three *Indiana Jones* features, six *Star Wars* episodes, and at least six *Batman* films. Sequels are testaments to the fact that we can never get enough of a good story.

If you have been successful in your **7-Slide Solution™** presentation, then the same dynamic will be present. While the resolution scene tied up "loose ends" and answered the questions raised during the story, it didn't resolve all the questions that are floating around in the minds of the audience.

The goal of slide 7 is to set up the sequel – the additional stories that your original story is likely to generate. These are the stories that audience members began composing in their heads as soon as you began presenting. This chapter gives you the techniques for constructing the seventh slide.

Let the Audience Take Control, Sort Of

Your job as the *active* presenter and storyteller is over, for a moment. You have put your best thoughts on the table in a dramatic and concise way. You have raised questions and answered them. You have supplied the facts that are needed to support your ideas. You have created some emotional resonance to motivate the audience to make a decision.

Somewhere in time, business and professional people developed the belief that a good presentation should leave no questions unanswered. This notion says that a presenter must address every contingency, all possibilities, provide every shred of evidence – leave no stone unturned. No wonder so many presentations veer out of control.

The truth is good ideas raise as many questions as they answer. They bring new conflicts to the surface. Each of those conflicts has the potential to be the basis for another story. Which raises additional conflicts. Which leads to additional stories. It never ends. We *love* it.

Making Your Story My Story

"We are satisfied, as observers of actions, when the stories we hear match our own stories. When the match is very similar, we tell our version of the story. When the match is hardly a match at all, when we have a contradictory story, we tell it. Actually, the middle cases are the most interesting - when we have no story to tell. What do we do then? We look for one. We do this by asking ourselves questions."

Roger C. Schank
Northwestern University

Questions are important. They prove that the audience is interested in what you have to say and wants to see what happens next. Unanswered questions encourage audience members to develop their own stories to answer those questions. Some of the questions may be supportive of your ideas, some opposed.

While you can't control what people think, you can influence how they think about things. It is better to influence the way people structure their questions than to leave the process entirely in their hands. Slide 7 can be thought of as the audience participation moment. The audience gets the chance to direct the storyline to answer questions or challenge your approach – but *only* within the parameters that you establish.

Fill in the Blanks

Every presentation I have ever presented, witnessed, or advised on contains blanks – the gaps that exist to facilitate communication or streamline the story. To some audience members, these blanks are insignificant; to others, the blanks must be filled before they can make a decision.

No matter how well you know your audience, it is impossible to anticipate and then fill all of the needs of each audience member within the storyline. Presenters who attempt this task end by delivering presentations that are so lengthy that no one is satisfied, and the stories become hopelessly bogged down.

Still, you do not want any unresolved conflicts or hard-to-answer questions swimming around in audience members' heads. Slide 7 provides an opportunity to lead audience members to the related stories that further your ideas.

The questions that arise from business presentations always relate either to the *past* ("How did we get here?") or the *future* ("Where are we going?"). Questions about the past often relate to process. How did the presenter reach these conclusions? What research was conducted? How was it conducted? Who participated? They hint that the audience is not totally satisfied. The future questions relate to possibilities. What's the best that can happen? How do we make this happen? What's the worst that can happen? These questions indicate general acceptance and enthusiasm.

Questions as Scorecard

One way to tell if your presentation has been successful is to gauge the questions audience members ask.

1. If most questions are about the future, you have succeeded. The audience still wants to see what happens next…

2. If most questions are about the past, you probably have more work to do. The audience wants backstory.

If a business story has been successful, most of the questions will be future-oriented. If less successful, a combination of past and future. If a failure, all about the past.

Put the Lid on the Can of Worms

Countless hours of thought and endless numbers of pages have been dedicated to understanding the dynamics of group behavior. Suffice to say, people behave differently in groups than in one-to-one situations. As a presenter, it's your job to manage that behavior.

Because of group dynamics, every presenter is faced with the legendary "can of worms" conflict – encouraging questions without losing control of the message vs. discouraging questions and not providing the audience with enough information to make a decision.

That's why slide 7 should be reserved to frame the questions for the audience. To set up this slide with the audience, a presenter might say something like: "I would like to go straight to the action plan, but I realize that you may want to know some more about how I arrived at the conclusion … how would you like to proceed?"

Decision Support Tools

Action Plan/Time Line

Methodology   Likely Stakeholder Responses

Sources and References   Best/Worse Case Scenarios

Cost/Productivity Calculations   Forecasts/Projections

This slide concludes the presentation about the Customer Service conflict with a series of links related to possible areas of inquiry that the audience may raise. This slide attempts to manage the audience's questions so that they relate to both the past (methodology, sources and references, and calculations) and the future (stakeholder responses, best/worst case scenarios, and forecasts and projections). Most importantly, it directs the audience to consider the ultimate future-oriented question – the action plan.

Each topic is linked to another story. For example, the methodology link could launch 7 slides or *less* describing a research premise, the core conflict inherent in getting to the truth, tension, turning point and resolution. Similar stories could be developed for the other topics.

Some people might say that a slide like this opens a can of worms by inviting questions and objections after the resolution has been presented. If the audience seems satisfied and content with your resolution – why not leave it at that?

I agree. *If* the audience appears satisfied. There are very few stories that are so compelling that audience members sit in hypnotic compliance with every point the presenter makes. By anticipating questions and offering to answer them, slide 7 can help you accomplish at least five things:

1. Avoid confusing the main story with a lot of backstory, asides, or other distractions.
2. Exert influence on the *way* people think about the story. People like

to have their choices laid out for them and will only challenge obviously self-serving approaches.

3. Fill in the blanks that you left out of the main story for the sake of dramatic impact and brevity.

4. Avoid the questions and objections that may damage your objectives. There is no guarantee that those questions won't come up, but you may be able to steer the audience away from those points by focusing the group on the questions and issues that you are prepared to address.

5. Demonstrate how hard you worked and how smart you are.

What if the audience really seems persuaded at slide 6? Really seems convinced that the resolution offered is right for them? If that's the case, the answer is simple – *do not use this slide*. If you can employ the **7-Slide Solution™** in six, or five or even one slide, then you have my complete respect. However if you're concerned that your story may raise questions, then the best way to answer a question is with another story.

Principles of Slide 7

The goal of encouraging the audience to want to see what happens next doesn't always end at resolution – that desire may extend beyond the story line. The best sequel to any presentation answers the question "How do we get the idea done?" However, the professional presenter is prepared to frame other questions that may arise: questions about the data and insights that led to the conclusions.

One key difference between the **7-Slide Solution™** and many presentations I have seen is that this process lets the audience drive the areas of inquiry instead of trying to force anticipated questions and answers into the storyline.

Principles of Slide 7

1. Let the audience drive the story by choosing topics to explore further.

2. Influence the way people think about your story by offering answers to questions before they are asked.

3. Answer each anticipated question with a story (premise, conflict, tension, turning point, resolution).

4. If you don't need slide 7, don't use it.

Slide 7 frames the questions that may be asked and influences the audience's topics of discussion. In the 2004 U.S. Presidential election, journalists, talking heads, and others noted that 26% of voters indicated that "moral values" played a major role in their voting decision. That insight came from a polling survey that offered prompted, multiple-choice answers. When asked to give answers to the factors that influenced them without prompts, the moral values issue was cited much less often. How questions are posed affects how people come to conclusions.

Most stories start with a question – "What would happen if...?" One of the best ways to answer interesting questions is with an interesting story. Using slide 7 to set up the sequel to your story is the same as using slide 2 for backstory – if you don't need it, don't use it. Prepare it anyway. Remember that the **7-Slide Solution™** is like golf – the lower your score, the better.

Chapter 22
Putting It All Together

Seven slides. Seven roles. Each slide in the **7-Slide Solution™** can be designed to elicit an intellectual and emotional response from your audience.

Like a scene in a play or movie, each slide plants a question, evokes an emotion, answers the question, and moves the story forward.

Just as with a good story, the audience is hooked by conflict in the first slide – engagement. The presenter kindles the desire to see what happens next early and keeps it going throughout the presentation.

There is one goal for the opening slide – to engage the audience. That means providing facts to start the decision-making process, while evoking emotions to motivate people to make the right decisions.

In the Customer Service example, slide 1 establishes the core conflict by planting the question,

---

The Role of Each Slide in the 7-Slide Solution™

Slide 1 - Engagement

Slide 2 - Backstory

Slide 3 - Build Tension

Slide 4 - Bring it to a boil

Slide 5 - Offer choice(s)

Slide 6 - Provide resolution

Slide 7 - Set up the "sequel"

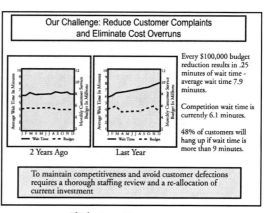

Slide 1 – Engagement

"How do we manage our operating costs while reducing wait times and improving customer satisfaction?" This evokes some emotions in the audience – primarily fear – by showing how our loss of competitiveness may result in a loss of business.

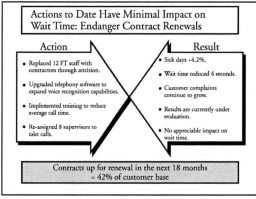

Slide 2 – Backstory

Depending on your knowledge of the audience, slide 2 can be used to provide the right amount of background information that will make the audience comfortable and willing to hear the rest of the story. This is called backstory. The challenge is to create a backstory that is interesting, without being so interesting that it competes with the main story.

Like any good backstory scene, this example plants and then answers the question – "how did we get here?" It doesn't ignore emotion, however. It provides troublesome facts and a dramatic bridge to the next slide.

Slide 3 builds tension by demonstrating the "insistence" of our action vs. the "resistance" of declining results. Once again, the desire to see what happens next is maintained by emphasizing the potential for reduced contract renewals.

Slide 3 – Build Tension

Tension is brought to a boiling point by adding one more powerful consequence. This consequence brings pressure on the audience to move from considering information to acting on it.

146

The strategy in slide 4 is to build the tension to the point so that the audience begins searching for resolution. In this case, the competitive threat is real and the implications of not taking action are obvious. The goal is to raise the tension – but not too much.

Tension is only relieved when someone makes a decision. Slide 5 offers a choice. Usually that choice is an either/or proposition between maintaining the status quo (with some revisions) or considering a substantial change. Slide 5 works to frame the decision in ways that you, as the presenter, want it framed. In this case, maintain the status quo and stagnate *or* consider a new way and open up opportunities.

Slide 6 provides resolution to the conflict that engaged the audience at the start. The best resolutions allow the audience to "have their cake and eat it, too." The principles for this slide are:

    1.   Resolve the core conflict

Slide 4 – Bring to a Boil

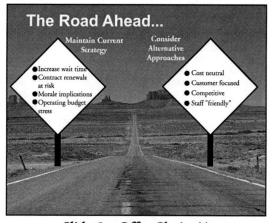

Slide 5 – Offer Choice(s)

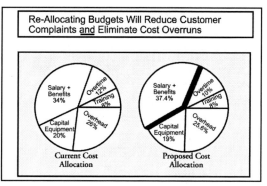

Slide 6 – Provide Resolution

2. Answer questions the story raised
3. Focus on "what", let them *ask* "how"
4. Show, don't tell

This resolution slide responds to the questions, challenges, or claims made in slide 1. It shows how a budget re-alignment will allow the Customer Service department to hire sufficient personnel so that wait times will be reduced – at the current budget guidelines.

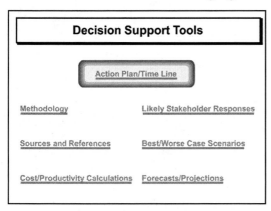

Slide 7 – Set up the "Sequel"

The seventh slide sets up the sequel. It directs the audience to ask questions about the past (the left side of this slide). These are questions the presenter hopes they don't ask because they demonstrate possible doubt. It also frames answers to questions about the future (on the right side of this slide). These are the questions the presenter wants because they demonstrate general acceptance of the story.

The **7-Slide Solution™** is more than a presentation strategy. It is a communication platform designed to accommodate the way people think. The cognitive science is clear. People are not fact processors. Most facts and statistics leave our memories before we leave the presentation. So professionals are constantly seeking ways to communicate more efficiently and effectively. For decades, the solution has been technological: telephony, wireless, e-mail, Wi-Fi. And, of course, PowerPoint®. The results have been mixed. We can communicate faster and more extensively than ever before. Books, music, videos and just about any other form of information can be broken down into 0's and 1's and disseminated anywhere in the world. Still, some of us worry that we aren't getting the precise information required to make decisions. All of us want a method to grab hold of and interpret ideas so that we can find some meaning through all of the noise and clutter. Isn't it ironic that the method has nothing to do with technology and is, instead, something as simple and ancient as a story?

Chapter 23
Using the 7-Slide Solution™ for Review and Update Meetings

Many of the 30 million presentations that take place each day in the U.S. are dedicated to updates and progress reviews: how are resources being allocated and what results are being achieved? During all of these meetings, presenters want to put their best foot forward and show that they are on top of things.

Often these presentations are data-laden affairs recapping the past in an endless series of charts and graphs. Some presenters argue that there is no other way to handle this type of meeting – that there really is no "story" in a business review. My argument is the opposite: that these meetings should be designed and constructed as real stories that show how a conflict has been addressed (or not addressed) and what the future can be.

The Stories Behind Reviews and Updates

With modern technology, we can access data by punching a few keys and looking at a screen. It can be cross-referenced and modeled and interpreted in dozens of ways with the click of a mouse. If managers want sales data, or productivity statistics, or inventory levels, then they do not need to call a meeting. However, they do need the story behind the facts – what's actually happening on the ground. What is really involved to perform a job? How do people feel about a new policy or practice? What hurdles must be overcome?

149

Management reviews are about *human* activities. Updates are about the results of *people's* efforts. Wherever there are people, there are conflicts. There is tension. There is a need for resolution. In short, a story.

Presenters who overlook the inherent drama in a management review or update are positioning themselves as more extensions of technology. Presenters who grasp that it's all about the human side of things make themselves indispensable in interpreting what is really going on.

Resonance, Not Re-Caps

In the United States, a good example of an update is the President's annual State of the Union address.

Article 2, Section 3 of the United States Constitution states: "[The President] shall from time to time give to the Congress information of the State of the Union and recommend to their Consideration such Measures as he shall judge necessary and expedient."

In the past, Presidents followed the letter of the law and provided information documents to the Congress without actually making a speech. Others recognized this review as an opportunity to tell their story and create an environment for change. The Monroe Doctrine, the "Four Freedoms," and the "Great Society" are some of the big ideas presented in State of the Union updates.

Review and update meetings are designed to answer the question, "How are we doing?" That question contains several more questions. How are we doing compared to what? Are we living up to expectations? Are we likely to exceed goals or sorely disappoint? It is a question that can be answered in one of two ways: by providing data that demonstrate results versus a set of goals, or, by creating a dramatic picture of how things are and what might be. In fact, because the audience is primed to think about performance in these kinds of meetings, then there may be no better time to create the kind of resonance that influences people to think and act differently.

Finding a Premise for Reviews and Updates

Answering the question "How are we doing?" is not just about the past and present. Most people care about how they are doing as it relates to their ability to do as well or better in the future. A budget update is not just about how much has been spent – it's about how much is *left* to spend in the future. A headcount review is not just about how many people were hired, it's about having the right resources to go forward.

Paradoxically, a review meeting is often the ideal time to talk about the future. The story structure – premise, core conflict, tension, turning point, resolution – can transform flat historical data into a compelling call to action by humanizing the information and building the desire to see what happens next.

> Things that are done, it is needless to speak about… things that are past, it is needless to blame.
>
> *Confucius*
> *Analects*

Strong premises for review stories mix lots of future with a bit of past. A story premise like "Demonstrate opportunities to overcome obstacles" or "Explain strategies for building momentum based on current trends" imposes a responsibility on the presenter to move out of the past/present and put the spotlight where the audience wants it to be – on the future.

Conflict and Tension – In a Business Review?

Having sat through my share of dry, monotonous business reviews, I can understand that you may be skeptical. "Is there a really a way to inject some conflict and tension into these kind of presentations?"

History is more than a review of dates and events. It resonates when we understand the conflicts and tension that resulted. Knowing that a major interna-

Conflicts Inherent in Most Reviews/Updates

1. Past vs. Future
2. Goals vs. Obstacles
3. Opportunity vs. Risk
4. Cost Containment vs. Growth
5. Investment vs. "milking"

tional incident involving nuclear missiles occurred between the US and USSR during October 1962 provides the basic facts of the Cuban Missile Crisis. Knowing the players (Kennedy, Castro, Khrushchev) and how close the world was to nuclear war and how everyday citizens reacted brings the story to life.

Your review or update presentations may not reach the emotional resonance of an international crisis. However when there are results, there are always some conflicts inherent in *how* those results were achieved. Answering questions like the ones below can uncover the conflicts and tension you need to make a review or update meeting come alive:

1. When the goals were set for the activity being reviewed, what real-world considerations were (or were not) considered?
2. What were conditions when the goals were established? What are conditions now?

3. What internal and/or external obstacles had to be overcome (or remain to be overcome) in order for these results to be achieved?

4. What factors would have contributed to making these results even better (or at least tolerable)?

5. What can happen if the conditions that contributed to these results don't change?

6. What errors in judgment contributed to these results?

7. How much did luck (good or bad) contribute to these results?

8. What emotional factors (like fear, complacency or arrogance) contributed to these results?

9. What previously unknowable factors (like natural disasters or competitive strategies) contribute to these results?

10. What are the best/worse case scenarios for the future?

The situation that you are called to review and update is the result of conflicts overcome and tensions relieved. De-constructing results to show how they were achieved is the difference between a compelling story and a dull recitation of past events. Historical stories and movies are interesting to us even though we know "how they end" because they reveal new dimensions by raising and resolving conflicts. Your review presentations can have the same impact.

Universal Resolution

In a business review meeting, the obvious resolution is to build on the things done right and avoid repeating the things done wrong. That's why it's important in an update presentation to move quickly from past performance to future opportunities. When the results being reported are positive, the resolution should show how the "good" could be maintained and enhanced in the future. If the results are less than hoped, the resolution should demonstrate how more positive results could be achieved.

Slide 1: Engagement

The audience expects to review performance, so the first slide must tell what has been happening. It should also set the stage to explore future possibilities. The connection with the audience is built by describing the conflict between what has happened and what is possible. The core conflict primes the audience to consider that, even if the goals were realized or mistakes were made, there are still some opportunities.

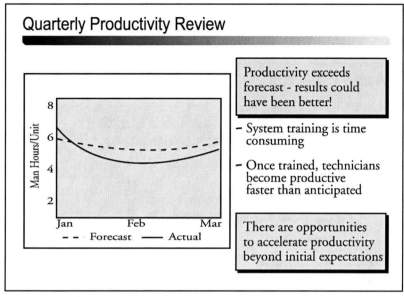

This slide reviews productivity for the first quarter in terms of man-hours per unit produced. The information is positive because the team is working less than six hours on each unit. The presenter could have rested on his or her laurels and accepted congratulations. Instead, conflict and tension are induced: "Results could have been better."

This slide follows the scene structure:

1. It raises a question – "How are we doing?"
2. It evokes and emotion - "Could we do better?"
3. It answers the question – results are above forecast and greater productivity has been achieved.
4. It moves the story forward – opportunities to accelerate productivity exist.

This slide is both quantitative (results vs. forecast) and qualitative (we could do better). It provides productivity data that is, presumably, available elsewhere, and enhances it with the presenter's perspective. It creates the desire to see what happens next by hinting at opportunities.

Slide 2: Backstory

Many people think that a business update is nothing but backstory. After all, the one and only backstory question is "How did we get here?"

That is what most people expect of a review meeting. However, a successful review meeting not only explains how we got here *but* where we are going.

In review presentations, the backstory slide (or slides, if necessary) reflect the changes made since the last update and how those changes have impacted results.

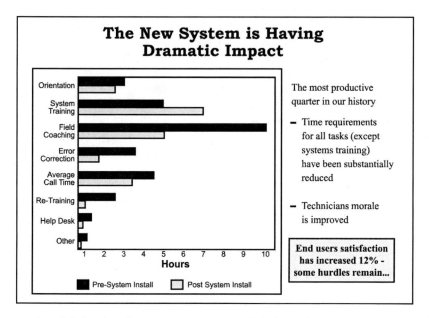

This slide bridges from the engagement slide by linking the positive productivity to a new system and evokes an emotion of pride by stating that the quarter is the most productive in history. It quickly summarizes the productivity gains in a number of dimensions (orientation, coaching, etc.) and moves the story forward with the tagline, "some hurdles remain."

An additional backstory slide may be necessary, depending on audience expectations and the extent of the update.

Slide 3: Build Tension

Whether the news is good or bad, building tension in a review presentation has a positive impact. Generally, that means examining the factors that are impeding better performance. The overall goal is to instill a level of dissatisfaction with current results in order to create a more receptive climate for the recommended changes to come.

To continue the productivity review, this slide introduces some cause for concern: "What costs have been incurred to realize the productivity gain?"

It again evokes an emotion of pride – recruiting and system training is exceeding projections. It answers the question by stating that re-training (and the costs incurred) is becoming virtually unnecessary. It bridges to the next slide with the mysterious "but..."

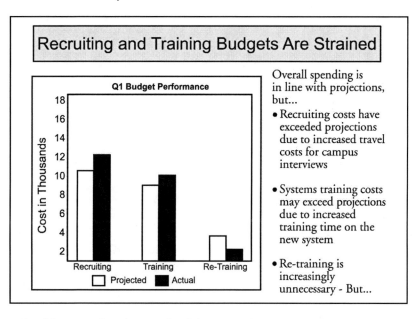

In this example, the productivity news is encouraging, so injecting a cause for concern and then resolving that concern can be a good strategy. If the news is mostly bad, then the tension slide can raise the question "What if it gets worse?" It can then evoke emotions of further loss and answer the question with a bridge to the next slide.

Slide 4: Bring it to a Boil

If the results under review are positive, then the presenter can bring a message to a boil by examining the opportunities to exceed expectations. This slide can ask the question "What if we really stretch to succeed?" It can evoke the emotions of gain and pride. It can answer the question by offering possible changes to remove the remaining obstacles and automatically bridge to the next slide by offering a preview of such sunny possibilities.

If the results under review are negative, then the boiling point can be reached by posing the question, "What if things get worse?" It can evoke the emotions of fear and insecurity. It can answer the questions by offering a way to overcome some of the obstacles and barriers.

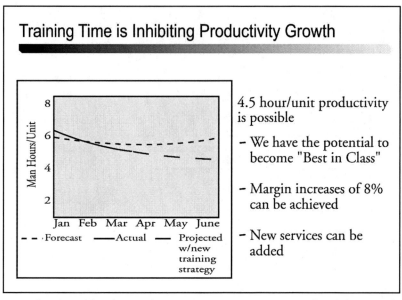

In this example, the productivity story is positive, so the slide is used to push for further gains. It connects from the tension slide by asking the question, "What do more system training and tougher recruiting mean to the organization?" It evokes the emotion of potentially lost opportunities in margin growth and best in class status. It answers the question by stating that further productivity gains are possible as well as an interesting reference to "new services." The slide bridges to the next one by putting it to the audience with the tagline "So…"

Without the audience realizing it, this review meeting is fast becoming a strategy session. The emphasis has moved from the past to the future. They are about to be asked to make decisions.

Slide 5: Offer Choices

In a review meeting, tension is relieved by offering a simple choice – are we content with living with the results as they are *or* do we want to examine ways to make them better?

This slide presents the choice in stark simplicity. Because the productivity results are positive in this example, the emotional appeal is to gain and further growth. If the results were negative, then the presenter could appeal to the dangers of doing nothing. Either way, the audience members are no longer passive consumers of historical data: they must take a position and consider change.

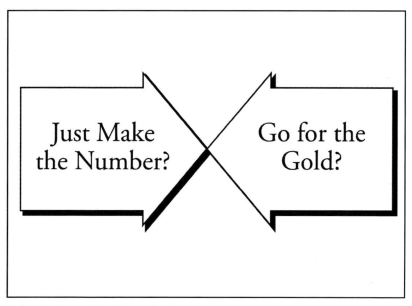

Slide 6: Provide Resolution

In an update presentation, the resolution slide has one of two goals: to maintain or expand the positive results under review *or* offer ways to minimize or eliminate the negative results.

This slide raises the question, "Can we have our cake and eat it too?" It raises emotions of hopefulness and confidence. It answers the question by providing a conceptual way to overcome obstacles.

Go for the Gold in Q2

☑ Reduce recruiting costs by 22%

☑ Compress systems training time 5 hours

☑ Eliminate re-training

Recommendations

• Recruit from the competition, not just campuses

• Add part time training coordinator

• Improve testing

This resolution slide provides a road map for achieving further productivity gains by resolving the conflict of extra training time to realize improved productivity.

The audience members have been briefed on the results to date and offered an opportunity to attain even better results in the future. The presenter has successfully moved the focus from the past to the future and elevated the discussion from a data review to a real strategy session.

Slide 7: Set Up the Sequel

If the story is well told, the seventh slide may be unnecessary. If it is necessary, then here are some of the additional stories you may want to link:

1. In-depth analysis of results
2. A review of the methodology used
3. Cost calculations
4. Examples and models

It all starts with attitude. If you believe your role is simply to communicate data, then the 7-**Slide Solution™** will not be helpful in a review or update meeting. If you accept the idea that meetings are to review progress and activities are truly opportunities to share new ideas and move your agenda forward, then the 7-**Slide Solution™** can revolutionize the way you think about and deliver these presentations.

Chapter 24
Using the 7-Slide Solution™ with Contractors, Agencies, Service Providers, and Other Third Parties

Around the world, organizations are increasingly focusing on their core competencies and outsourcing just about everything else. Service providers as varied as IBM and small Mom & Pop design shops have become almost like family to large organizations.

While most contractors and other service providers try hard to integrate into their clients' culture, they remain separate entities with separate cultures, practices, and ways of doing business.

Usually, these service providers have other clients making different demands on their time, resources, and attention. The result is that communication between contracting organizations and their third party service providers can sometimes be frustrating. Jargon must be explained, business practices and values must be reinforced, and some, but not all, information must be shared. The inevitable grinding at the organizational boundaries is bound to cause friction between presenters who are directing outside resources and the audiences who provide those functions.

When people interact with third party resources, they have a communications dilemma. They must keep their partners in the loop so that the work will be done to the highest possible standards, but the contractor simply does not have the time or interest that an insider does. How much information and knowledge about the client organization is necessary to do the job? How interested is the third party in knowing about the client?

It's the age-old problem – what to leave in, what to leave out. Just the kind of problem the **7-Slide Solution™** is designed to address.

Developing a Premise for a Third Party Presentation

While each presentation will address different issues, there are some principles that can be applied in making presentations to third parties:

1. *It's all about "we":* It is important to be inclusive and share responsibility for problems and kudos for successes. There is often a desire to blame contractors and take a boss/subordinate approach. Although many third party providers appear to accept this approach, they can be deeply resentful.

2. *Pride carries heavy resonance:* For most service providers, their greatest asset is their reputations. If you are looking for an emotion to tap for resonance, look no further than pride. Pride of accomplishment. Pride of reputation. Pride of affiliation.

3. *Show, Don't Tell:* Third party suppliers know their businesses, and know what their roles are in helping client organizations to reach their objectives. When confronted with powerful messages, most will respond professionally.

4. *Focus on the end-user:* While the client has every right to demand the performance, focusing on the ultimate customers or end-users who will benefit from the services provided takes a little of the "us vs. them" dynamic out of the presentation. If the provider is an IT contractor, focus the premise on the people who will use the system. If an ad agency is the audience, then build the premise on the needs of your customers.

5. *What's in it for the contractor?:* It's easy to direct the premise solely on your needs and the needs of the end user. However, your third party service providers are businesses. There should be "a little somethin' in it for them" as well. Whether it's financial gain, increased visibility, prestige, or a chance at future contracts, blend some benefits into the premise.

Finding Conflict and Tension – Not as Easy as You Might Think

If you work with third party service providers you may be thinking, "Conflict is only a phone call away." It's usually possible to find something unpleasant in the relationship between companies and contractors.

The core conflicts that will hook third party service providers relate to the issues that keep them up at night. Issues like delivering better service vs. incurring additional costs, or offering creative solutions vs. towing the corporate line. If you can find conflicts that relate to the provider's business and, when resolved, can help your end-users, then you have a winning story to tell.

Collaborative Resolutions

The stories you present to third party providers are about them – and about you and your end-users. When resolving the core conflict, remember to include yourself as part of the resolution.

Slide 1: Engagement

To engage an audience that must pay attention to you – and to its other clients and demands – illustrate a conflict that has the potential to impact all three parties: the client organization (you), the end users (your customers) and the third party provider or contractor. The thrust can be positive about the opportunities that exist or negative about the problems to be overcome.

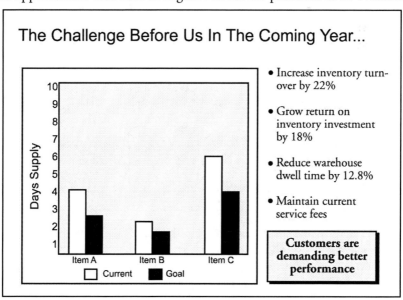

The overall message should be one of collaboration and the need to build a consensus about what to do.

For this chapter, the example presentation is made by a manufacturing company to an outsourced logistics company that handles transportation and warehousing of the company's finished goods. The manufacturer is under pressure to reduce inventories at its largest customer and must enlist the contractor's help to streamline the supply chain.

This engagement slide does not point fingers or seek to assign blame: it hooks the audience with a challenge. The audience members may be uneasy if the numbers are an aggressive stretch, or curious as to how the presenter intends to accomplish these objectives. One thing is certain – they will be engaged.

Slide 2: Backstory

When presenting to third parties, a good backstory puts the focus on the end users and examines how the end users or customers "got here." This approach minimizes the "us vs. them" dynamic and shines attention where it belongs – on solving the end user's problems.

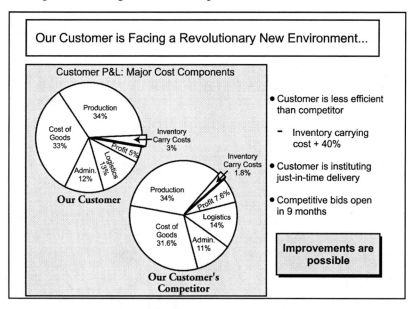

In this slide, the focus is entirely on the customer. The higher costs of doing business – especially inventory carrying costs – are forcing changes that both the manufacturer and the logistics contractor must address if they want to satisfy the ultimate customer and retain the business.

A sense of urgency is established by pointing out that the manufacturer's agreement with the customer is up for bid in nine months. A sense of opportunity as well as a bridge to the next slide is provided with the tagline "improvements are possible..."

This slide says nothing about the relationship between the manufacturer and the logistics contractor. It answers the question, "How did we get here?" by demonstrating the *customer's* situation and demands.

Slide 3: Build Tension

At slide 3, the presenter should start to examine how the relationship between the two organizations is affecting the performance of the end user. This can be tricky: there is often a fine line between exploring opportunities for improvement and finger pointing. The goal is not to create tensions between the organizations but to demonstrate that if nothing is done, *both* organizations stand to lose.

The contractor is caught between two forces – the organization that is the client and pays the bills and the end-users (the clients of the client). Companies which purchase outside services can (and too often do) squeeze the contractor by saying, "It's your fault — fix it." A better approach is to demonstrate the impact of the tension on *both* organizations in order to create a collaborative environment to seek resolution.

In this slide the challenge is laid out in graphic detail. The major bottleneck is in the third party contractor's warehouse.

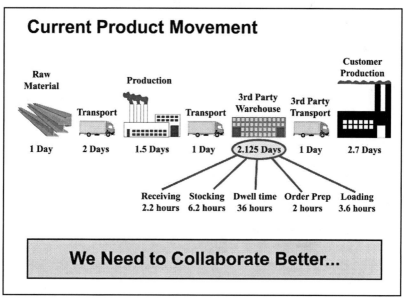

The slide asks the question, "Where are we slowing down?" It taps into a fear of loss by implying that the current movement is unacceptable to the customer. It answers the question by *showing* the situation, not telling. Each link in the supply chain is delineated and the area of concern is highlighted. It keeps the story moving forward by admitting that collaboration could be better.

Slide 4: Bring it to a Boil

When presenting to third party service providers, the consequences of not resolving the core conflict will generally fall into one of three categories:

1. *End-user displeasure:* Complaints will rise, usage will decline, revenues will slip, etc. However, this may not resonate if the third party contractor's work is at such a distance from the end user that it isn't "personal."

2. *Contractual threats:* The relationship may be "re-thought," penalties may be imposed, other options may be considered. This can be effective with smaller contractors, but it is unlikely to hold much water with big IT contractors or accounting or legal firms that are firmly entrenched with the corporate office.

3. *Mutually Assured Destruction (MAD):* The Cold War strategy that recognizes that both organizations stand to lose. This is usually effective, regardless of the size and strength of the contractor.

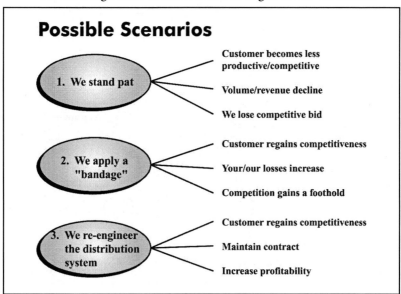

This slide provides a number of scenarios to answer the question "What if we don't respond to the core conflict?" It raises emotions of potential loss of business, reputation, and profitability. It answers the question by offering to collaborate on "re-engineering" the distribution system. No tagline is necessary. The audience members will ask – "How?" and want to see what happens next...

Slide 5: Offer Choice(s)

The turning point slide – slide 5 – may not always be necessary in a third party presentation. That's because the contractor knows the terms of the contract and knows the possible consequences of not resolving conflicts. It may be possible to go straight from the boiling point to resolution.

If you decide to offer a choice, it can be very stark – work to make things better or suffer the consequences. Or, it can be more conciliatory – "Do you want to hear my resolution or do you have one?"

Strategic Options

1. Collaborate to reach efficiency goals in a cost-neutral way

2. Return to direct distribution

3. Seek other partners

> **There's still time to compete**

In this case, the presenter has taken a matter-of-fact approach by listing the strategic options available. Two of the choices are unattractive to the contractor, so collaboration is the only option.

Slide 6: Resolution

The major point to remember when resolving a story with third party service providers is that the resolution is a *joint* one. It should always include what the organization is willing to do as well as what it is requiring the contractor to do.

If the presentation has recognized that both organizations have contributed to the core conflict, then a joint resolution should not be that challenging. If the presentation has been aimed at assigning blame, such a resolution may be nearly impossible.

A Proposed Way Forward

IMPROVEMENT OPPORTUNITY	US	YOU
Receiving	36 hour advanced notification	Initiate Automated manpower scheduling
Stocking	Pre-sorted pallets	Assign specific warehouse location for JIT
Dwell Time	Improve demand forecasting with customer	Institute 24 hour shipment preparation procedures
Order Prep	Automate in conjunction with forecast	Access orders on-line
Loading	Pre-sorted pallets	Assign "SWOT" teams for rush orders

In this example, the resolution is a straightforward plan of action with responsibilities clearly delineated.

It follows the scene structure by asking the question, "How do we change?" The emotion is calm but insistent and the answers are the topline strategies – "topline" because it seeks conceptual agreement *before* drilling into the details. If the audience members accept the topline view, they will want to see the details. Even if they don't accept the outline, they may still want to hear how the presenter arrived at this resolution. Either way, the desire to "see what happens next" remains intact.

Slide 7: Set Up the Sequel

With almost any story that requires change, the audience will be uneasy. At the same time, it's guaranteed that if the story has been successful, they will want to know more.

Slide 7 bridges to other stories - stories about the past (methodology, calculations, historical insights, etc.) or the future (action plans, budgets, etc.).

This slide lays out the question – "What else do you need to know?" The left side is dedicated to in-depth backstory – "How we got here." The right side is future oriented – "What do we need to do?"

Each "button" on the slide links to further 7-slide (or less) stories that the audience needs to know.

When working with agencies, contractors and other third party service providers, time is often at a premium. Attention may be limited as the contractor juggles multiple client commitments and priorities. Communication must be efficient, timely, and brief. It must also be concise, meaningful, and compelling enough to generate the right kind of action.

7-Slide Solution™

Chapter 25
Selling with the **7-Slide Solution**™

Selling is not only a matter of persuading people to buy products. It is also about creating long-term partnerships. It's not enough to sell a product or service: the seller must explain – convincingly – how his or her company will stand behind that product or service in terms of responsiveness, support, risk sharing, and a range of other intangibles. In other words, sales require selling *stories*.

The Story About Differentiation

For many manufacturing organizations, global sourcing of parts and limited R&D budgets is making product differentiation difficult. A few auto parts manufacturers make nearly all the components of cars sold in the world.

It's not much different for services. If a financial firm launches a successful new investment vehicle, then it's replicated within days.

With limited differences between products or services, what tips the scales in favor of one supplier over another? The seller's story.

Every company has a story. Some are better at telling theirs than others. In many industries, to "compete" means to add value, and sales people are expected to exemplify that added value personally. It's not so much about the consumer product as it is about the shoppers who will buy the product and what those shoppers mean to a retailer. It's not so much about the business service as it is about how that service can evolve and change as the client changes.

Developing a Premise for a Sales Story

An effective selling premise should include two critical components:

1. Identify how the prospective buyer's situation can be improved.
2. Demonstrate how the seller's company can address the improvement better than anyone else.

At their best, sales stories are not about products or services but about partners working together to achieve common interests.

It is in selling situations that the dilemma of *what to leave in, what to leave out* can be most troubling. Salespeople may only have one shot at an important decision maker. They may feel that a complete review of the seller's capabilities is warranted – the risk of missing a key point is just too great.

There are few communication arenas where the need to be concise and compelling is as important as in the sales arena. A well-told sales story provides benefits for both the seller and the prospective customer:

- It shows that the seller understands the customer. A salesperson who cuts through the noise and gets to the nub of a problem is the kind of person customers want to work with.
- It is efficient. It says to the customer, "I'm not here to waste your time."
- It differentiates. Competitors will often over-sell in the forlorn hope that they can overwhelm a buyer into acceptance.
- It demonstrates a level of confidence that says, "I understand your challenges and I'm ready to help address them."

The premise of a powerful sales story is about solving a problem for the prospective customer – perhaps a problem that the customer was not fully aware of (you never think about insurance until you have an accident or loss) – and developing a relationship that will make sure that the problem remains solved.

Looking at Conflict and Tension From the Other Side of the Desk

The language of selling reflects that the discipline is all about influencing people to make *decisions*. "Assume the close," "overcome the objections," "close the deal."

The evidence is clear that decisions are not made due to overwhelming logic, historical precedent, or even the possibility of rewards. Decisions are made when customers resolve conflicts. Conflicts between price and value, risk and reward, short-term vs. long-term. If a salesperson can identify the core conflict and then resolve it (or, at least, contribute to resolving it), that person will succeed most of the time.

To develop a successful **7-Slide Solution™** to a selling challenge, the seller must find and communicate the customer's core conflict in a given situation – the *customer's* core conflict. Too many salespeople think selling is about showing how their company is better than the competition. Or how their price is lower than anyone else's. Or how their products out-perform similar products. Those factors are important only if they resolve a conflict that the customer is experiencing.

A successful sales story starts by answering these questions:

1. What is keeping the prospective customer up at night?
2. What are the customer's options? Are they equally attractive?
3. Does the customer see the conflict the way I want him or her to see it?
4. How can I convince the customer to see the conflict the way I see it?

Looking at the conflict entirely from the customer's perspective makes the story more compelling and, ultimately, more successful.

Resolution: The Conditional Close

In most high-value sales situations (where substantial amounts of money are at stake), there is a conceptual buy-in before there is an actual order or signature on the paperwork. A successful sales story reaches resolution when the prospect is persuaded that the seller is the right resource. The final order may still require a proposal, negotiations, and reference checks, and sales can certainly go awry, even after a great sale story. However if agreement is established and confirmed at the resolution of the story, then the likelihood of success increases.

Slide 1 – Engagement

The engagement slide should "hook" the customer by demonstrating the seller's understanding of the issues the customer faces. It also begins the process of creating the seller's credibility as a resource to help meet those challenges.

The engagement slide should get to the point directly and succinctly and communicate that the seller will not waste the customer's time.

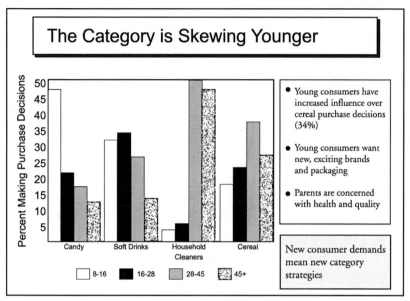

This is a presentation made by a breakfast cereal company to a major grocery chain. The cereal company is launching a new product and must persuade the retailer to stock the product to coincide with the start of a national advertising campaign. The seller knows that space on the shelf is scarce and that replacing an existing product with a new one won't sway the customer. A strong story is needed.

Rather than begin with a straight product pitch, the salesperson opens with information regarding the target consumer and changing shopping patterns. The strategy is to engage the customer on a larger trend, then show how the company is responding in product development.

This slide reflects the scene structure:

1. It raises a question – "How do I increase cereal sales?"
2. It evokes an emotion – is the customer keeping current with the latest trends – or missing opportunities?
3. It answers the question – young consumers have more influence in purchase decisions.
4. It moves the story forward – new demands require new strategies.

Slide 2: Backstory

This backstory slide introduces the product. It bridges from the previous slide by posing the question – "How is the company responding to developing consumer trends?" The answer uses research to explain how the product was developed and to reinforce the message that times are changing. Hinting that the customer's competitors are ready to get on board moves the story forward.

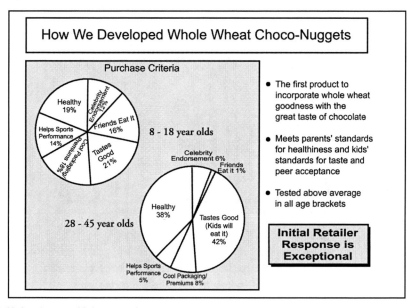

Slide 3: Build Tension

Tension can be built in a number of ways. In this case, the seller describes how the launch will take place and what resources are allocated to this product.

This approach poses the question, "What will you miss if you don't stock the product?" It raises the emotions related to possible lost opportunities and answers the question with a subtle but clear message – "get on board or risk losing out to your competition."

In effect, the seller is saying, "We're going ahead with or without you." The emotional resonance of being left behind can be quite strong.

The Whole Wheat Choco-Nuggets Launch Strategy

1. Stock 4 sizes of Whole Wheat Choco-Nuggets in all major grocery and discount chains

2. Free samples <u>and</u> coupons to 15 million households with incomes above $55,000

3. $50 Million advertising on Saturday cartoons and NFL Football

4. Special display incentives to grocery stores

> **There's still time to compete**

Slide 4: Bring it to a Boil

Slide 4 may be the most sensitive slide in a selling story. The seller must be careful not to appear manipulative by creating a false sense of urgency. However, stories are best told when the tension builds to a point where the audience is looking for relief.

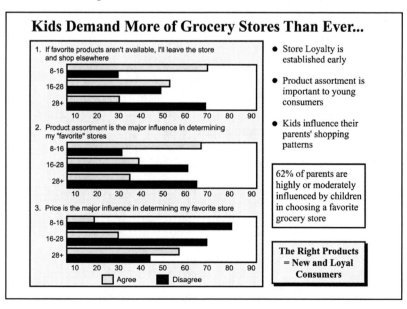

The trick is to find a balance between a sense that action is required soon without hinting that the customer is inept or incapable of seeing impending danger.

In this slide, the seller shifts the emphasis from the product to the customer's business. Specifically, the question is posed, "What if young consumers don't find the products they want?" This evokes an emotional response of some anxiety in the customer. The question is answered using data that shows store loyalty among younger consumers who will shop elsewhere if their products are not in stock.

The story is moved forward with a tagline that equates product range to consumer loyalty.

Slide 5: Offer Choice(s)

Slide 5 relieves the tension by offering a choice: stock the item or not. This choice is offered with a twist. It summarizes the pluses and minuses of the product and closes the scene with "You Decide…" This approach demonstrates confidence in the story (and the product): if the story is strong, then it can be an effective strategy for slide 5.

The Pluses and Minuses of Stocking Whole Wheat Choco-Nuggets

Pluses	Minuses
• Meet emerging consumer demands	• New concept - may not work
• Tie-in to the most extensive product launch in our history	• Take shelf space from existing items
• Become the store of choice for young consumers	• Unproven at store level
• Reinforce your "Healthy Foods" image	

You Decide…

Slide 6: Resolution

Resolution in a sales story is not the same as an order. In traditional selling terms, this slide is a "trial close" to gain agreement that the story makes sense, the seller is credible, and the customer is willing to take things to the next stage.

In this example, the seller continues the "get on board or get left behind" approach. The resolution is a summary of the company's plans for launching the product in the marketplace and asks – "Can we count on you?"

There is still a lot to be done —payment schedules, costs, specific incentives, etc. – but this resolution presumes a commitment before launching into the final closing information.

Slide 7: Set Up the Sequel

In a selling story, slide 7 plays a stronger role than it does in other presentations. While the conceptual framework may be agreed upon in slides 1 though 6, the "devil is in the details" and the customer will want to explore them before placing an order.

Using the left side of the slide for "past" issues and the right side for "future" concerns, this slide answers the question, "What else do you need to know?"

The customer may want to examine the supporting data or look forward to a plan of action.

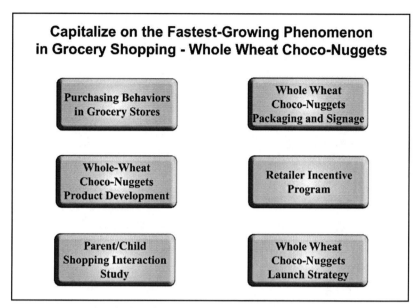

Customers who deal with salespeople on a regular basis have a special file for overblown, lengthy presentations that waste time and don't help them make informed decisions. It's called the "round file" (AKA garbage can) and it is the final resting place for much hard work by salespeople. Presenting a compelling sales story in 7 slides is not only considerate of the customer's time and attention; it's a real way to stand out from the crowd and generate sales.

Chapter 26
Making the **7-Slide Solution™** Part of Your Routine

Like taking on a new exercise routine or any other change of habit, following a new presentation platform requires some adjustments and effort.

In some organizations, incorporating the **7-Slide Solution™** may be made more difficult by organizational biases that reward windy, overblown presentations as somehow demonstrative of greater work effort.

Finally, because the **7-Slide Solution™** is about persuading audiences – and persuasion is far from a sure thing regardless of how a message is presented – an objective way to track changes in audience reception may help to measure your progress in making this platform work for you.

Getting Started: Think in Stories

It's simple: to use the **7-Slide Solution™**, think like a storyteller. Look for the elements of a good story in your everyday life. Observe your situation as a continuously unfolding story complete with premises, conflicts, tension, and resolution.

As you bring the storytelling techniques to your professional life, you should look for compelling premises that will resonate both intellectually and emotionally. Then find a strong core conflict on which to build the story and hook audience interest. From there, you can close the business story with a solid resolution.

To Create a Premise that Resonates

- Give equal weight to intellect and emotion
- Reverse engineer
- Use an emotion scale

The challenge is to find the resonance – the right balance of intellectual and emotional appeal within the story. One way to evoke resonance is to give both sides – intellectual and emotional – *equal* weight. Many business presenters are so uncomfortable with the emotional side of things that they add only a dash of emotion in a stew of intellect. Before you think about what you want to say, think about what you want the audience to *feel*. Do you want them to feel calm and confident or anxious and concerned? Cognitive scientists have determined that emotion is critical to effective decision-making. If the aim of your presentation is to influence the audience to make decisions (and if it isn't, then why are you presenting to them?) then make an emotional reaction a central goal.

A method that I use is to write the story and then "reverse engineer" it to find the most compelling premise and the sources of the resonance. Here's an example: suppose you are planning a budget review with your boss, the financial department, and other key managers. You could start by writing about what you know and sketch out a brief history. Something like this:

> "Beginning January 1, budgets were cut by 15% and headcount was reduced by one person. This put a much greater workload on the remaining staff; two people resigned before the end of February.
>
> We thought we could make up the difference by automating certain processes. That might have solved the problem except the IT vendor was late in installing the new system.
>
> We tried to recruit using the newspaper but the candidates were weak and we had to call in a recruiting firm. The firm found some good people and we made two hires by May 31.
>
> Meantime, overtime costs rose as people had to pick up the work of the three vacant positions (one reduction and two resignations).
>
> We forecast zero staff turnover so we didn't have an adequate budget for training costs. At this point, we have used the yearly allocation in the first half.
>
> The bottom line is we are 5% above budget."

Look at what you have written to isolate the most compelling premise and find where the resonance exists. To "reverse engineer" the story, simply go through the story and circle the premises and storylines. For example:

Beginning January 1, budgets were cut by 15% and headcount was reduced by one person. This put a much greater workload on the remaining staff; two people resigned before the end of February.

We thought we could make up the difference by automating certain processes. That might have solved the problem except the IT vendor was late in installing the new system.

We tried to recruit using the newspaper but the candidates were weak and we had to call in a recruiting firm. The firm found some good people and we made two hires by May 31.

Meantime, overtime costs rose as people had to pick up the work of the three vacant positions (one reduction and two resignations).

We forecast zero staff turnover so we didn't have an adequate budget for training costs. At this point, we have used the yearly allocation in the first half.

The bottom line is we are 5% above budget.

In this case, the reverse engineering process uncovered seven possible premises on which to build the story. The story could be about:

1. The effects of corporate budget cuts on operations
2. The domino effect of reducing headcount
3. Costs and problems of automating processes
4. Recruitment challenges
5. The hidden costs of austerity as they relate to overtime
6. The inability of the organization to reliably forecast staff movement
7. The challenge of budgeting training costs when staff turnover is unpredictable

Take a second look and determine which premise is the most emotionally interesting *to the audience* and apply a scale to it.

Keep in mind that the premise and the core conflict are intimately related. Some people start with the conflict and backtrack to the premise. That's perfectly alright if it works for you.

An Emotional Scale

5 = Borderline panic

4 = Itch that needs scratching

3 = Important but can wait a bit

2 = Interesting, but so what?

1 = Yawn!

Conflict is the essential element of good storytelling and there are literally thousands of examples surrounding you every day. Start with journalism: listen to a news radio station on your way to work or check out the newspaper. Filter out the facts and focus on the journalists' techniques. Pay close attention to the opening lines of a news report. Observe how conflicts are presented early in the story and how good journalists build tension.

Then, graduate to the pros of storytelling. Take a more critical look at your favorite drama or comedies on TV. Rent your favorite video and see how the director is "playing with your head" through the use of the story-telling techniques.

Before long you'll begin to see conflict everywhere and think of problem solving in a whole new light.

Discover Conflict

1. Look and listen
2. Take both sides of an argument
3. Think like the audience
4. The "versus" technique
5. Use default conflicts

Finally, transfer the techniques to your business life. When you plan a presentation or other communication, you will have a viewpoint on the best way to proceed. Take the time to develop a counter-argument and pursue it as aggressively as your preferred approach. For example, suppose a manager is convinced that a new method of processing incoming paperwork will improve productivity, reduce errors, and speed up response time. At the same time, this new method will require a delivery mechanism, staff training, and investment in new technology. By examining both sides of the argument – with equal passion – conflicts will float to the surface and the final communication will be better for it.

Perhaps the best way to find conflict is to think like the audience. Ask yourself, "What keeps them awake at night? What do they argue about among themselves?" Then ask yourself, "How can my story tap into those conflicts?" and more importantly, "How will my resolution contribute to their ability to resolve these conflicts?"

Another way to identify conflict is to step back and write the following on a piece of paper: "This presentation is *really* about _____ versus _____." Even the most complex communication challenges can usually be broken down to two essential but opposing concepts – x versus y.

There are a number of "default" conflicts in any business presentation. They include action vs. inaction, risk vs. rewards, save vs. invest, money vs. people, and right vs. wrong.

Finding a satisfying resolution to a story takes a unique combination of storytelling skill and technical knowledge in your particular field. It's one thing to know that "cake and eat it too resolutions" are the most satisfying. It's quite another to consistently come up with such resolutions.

Finding Resolution

- A complete resolution is not always necessary
- Take sides if you must
- Stay focused on the core conflict
- Keep it conceptual

Don't become so overwhelmed by the task of finding really innovative and dramatic resolutions to every business problem. No one can resolve *every* conflict every time. Be content to make a meaningful contribution to resolving bigger conflicts and your audience will respond positively.

If you can't find a "cake and eat it too resolution," then resolve one side of the conflict and argue it passionately. Audience members may disagree but at least they will appreciate that you see problems in more than one dimension.

Stories can "run away" from their authors. It happens to the best of them. Storylines are most often blurred when the storyteller loses focus on the core conflict. Your presentation is not meant to change the world. It *is* meant to pose a conflict, explore the implications, offer choices, and provide at least partial resolution. Stay focused on the core conflict and you are almost guaranteed to discover meaningful resolution.

Earlier you read of distinguishing between resolution and solutions. Your story should provide conceptual resolution to the core conflict without getting into every detail of a plan. Plans are great. You should definitely have one ready to follow up every presentation. But close the loop conceptually with your resolution before launching into the sequel of a detailed action plan.

Stopping Along the Way

Incorporating a new skill or way of doing things has two major components – mastery of the skill itself and mastery of the emotional hesitation of putting the skill to work.

It is overcoming the emotional hesitations that allow us to grow. Whether it's a new golf swing or accepting a new communication platform, the requirements are the same. Give it time. Practice. Evaluate. Practice some more.

People who work to make the **7-Slide Solution™** part of their routine face some of the hesitation that goes with trying anything new. These hesitations can be summarized into five areas.

Some Hesitations to Adopting the 7-Slide Solution™

1. Appearing unprepared
2. Choosing the wrong story
3. Executing poorly
4. "It's lonely out on this limb"
5. It doesn't feel safe

The first is appearing unprepared or under-prepared. The argument goes, "I can tell the story in 7 slides or less, but the audience is conditioned to think that more is better." The truth is: creating concise and meaningful communications involves more preparation than the meandering hodgepodges of information that often pass for business presentations. A sequel slide (slide 7) allows you to easily link to all the information the audience thinks it may be missing. The best way to overcome this hesitation will be the "proof in the pudding." You will be more confident using fewer slides when you observe people agreeing with your points, moving in the directions you want them to go, and just plain getting what you say to them.

The second hesitation is the fear of choosing the "wrong story." People worry that they will select the wrong premise or identify the wrong core conflict. In fact, there is no wrong story. You are the presenter and people come to the meeting to hear what you have to say. In most cases, you are the top expert in the room. There is no greater risk to your credibility and standing in the organization than trying to tell *every* possible story through a long and tedious data dump. Even if there were a wrong story, it would be far superior to most presentations that have no story at all.

A third worry is about poor execution. The argument goes, "It's hard enough to get my facts right and create the right visuals. I don't need to worry about having the right conflict or offering the right choices." That is like saying a blueprint for a house isn't important because it's too hard to get the lumber and concrete together. If you have done the work around the storyboard elements and you know what you are talking about, then you almost have to make an effort to fail.

Perhaps the greatest hesitation and the one most difficult to overcome harkens back to the adolescent fear of not fitting in –"Why should I be the only one doing this?"

It's a real concern. It is always easier to go along and do things like everyone else does. The easy road assumes that you are willing to be just as persuasive as everyone else, just as interesting as everyone else, just as *average* as everyone else. If you are really concerned about going

> "If the creator had a purpose in equipping us with a neck, he surely meant us to stick it out."
> Arthur Koestler
> *Novelist, Politician, Activist, Social Philosopher*

out on a limb, you may want to start with a few low-level presentations to peers or friendly customers and work your way up to the more complex presentations.

The final hesitation – "it doesn't feel safe" – is an easy one to address. First ask yourself, "Why should more slides make me feel more secure?" Is it because if you keep showing enough visuals, the audience may see a point where you don't? Do more slides allow you to keep talking until, odds are, something intelligent comes out? Do you believe that inanimate slides can tell a better story than a living, breathing human being? "Safety in numbers" does not apply to slides. Quite the opposite. Dangers lurk around every corner in overstuffed presentations. Dangers like boredom, selective exposure and misinterpretation. Dangers that are eliminated by the **7-Slide Solution™**.

Improvement is not easy. If it were, then everyone would do it. If you believe that some of the most important business communications can be improved and you can achieve more of your personal and business objectives through better communications, then overcoming personal challenges is a small price to pay.

A Personal Scorecard

The best way to make the **7-Slide Solution™** your routine is to watch the reactions of your audiences and determine the impact.

Will you dazzle every audience, every time? No.

Will you persuade people to think exactly like you on every issue, every time you present? Probably not.

Does that mean the **7-Slide Solution™** is not effective? Not at all.

Signs that the 7-Slide Solution™ Is Working
- Getting what you want
- Less call for repetition
- Clues of engagement
- Finishing early
- Questions about the future, not the past
- Less "nitpicking"
- Less resistance to controversy
- Using your "frames"

As you incorporate the **7-Slide Solution™** into your business meetings and presentations, it may be helpful to develop a scorecard to measure your progress and success.

The first and most important measure is: are you getting what you want? If your business stories deliver the results you seek, then you can still use some other measurements to enhance your presentations even further.

> "You can't always get what you want,
> But if you try sometimes
> You just may find
> You get want you need"
> *The Rolling Stones*

In those instances when you don't gain your goals, it's important to determine the extent of the impact of your story. Even if the audience does not accept your resolution, you will at least want to know that people are listening and seriously considering new ideas.

There are a number of ways to measure that impact. One way to know that your overall business story is clearly articulated is to notice how often you have to go back and review key elements of your presentation. It is common in business presentations for someone to ask, "Can you go back to the previous slide and take me through the numbers again…" The less frequently you receive questions like that, the more impact you have had as a presenter. Fewer repeats equal greater understanding, unless of course, you have so overwhelmed the audience that they are bored to numbness. So use this measurement in conjunction with the next…

…Behavioral "clues of engagement," or body language. Most people have a hard time concealing either interest or disinterest. If they are leaning forward in their seats, taking notes, or pausing for thoughtful silences, it means you are having an impact. They may not go along with all your thinking – but at least they are engaged.

I believe an early finish – *with satisfied audience members* – is the best indication that you have been persuasive. Always plan to finish early and stick to your plan. An important by-product of setting the goal to finish early is that it forces you to be even more concise and economical in your presentation.

Another indication that the **7-Slide Solution™** is working for you can be measured after you present the resolution of the story and set up the sequel (slide 7). If most of the questions pertain to the backstory – how you arrived at your conclusions, research methods and information sources, etc. – then that may be a sign of doubt and a warning that the story was not convincing. However, if most of the questions are about the future – next steps, action plans, responsibilities, etc. – then that is a good indication that people are interested and have accepted at least some of your ideas.

Most good presentations have controversial points that must be made. These points are always tense and can send the presentation into very positive problem solving directions or into utter chaos. Controversial topics combined with bad presentation design can be a lethal combination. If an audience is already bored and getting a bit "twitchy," then the controversial topic gives them the excuse they need to break the monotony, if for no other reason than to inject a little excitement into the gathering. On the other hand, a well-designed presentation already has conflict and tension "baked in," so the controversial topic may seem more like a logical part of the flow. Will the **7-Slide Solution™** make controversial issues non-controversial? Certainly not. However, if you recognize that such issues are generating even slightly less dramatic responses than you are used to, then you'll know that the process is working for you.

A final way to measure your persuasiveness is to plant "framing phrases" in your presentation. Then, after the presentation, see if attendees are using the phrases. For example, instead of using the term 'budget,' call it a "spending plan." See if e-mails, presentations, and informal conversations reflect these phrases. If they do, then give yourself a pat on the back for being persuasive.

Summary

I recognize that it is not easy to change a career full of practices and habits in the way you communicate to your customers and associates. However, sitting through poorly planned business presentations is a drain on your productivity. Creating and delivering a poorly planned presentation is borderline criminal. You know you don't like it – so why impose it on others?

As information proliferates and time becomes even more pressed, businesses and professional organizations may start imposing structural rules that may make matters worse. My greatest fear in writing this book is that some manager somewhere will look at the title, not read the book, and decree that "all presentation will henceforth be seven slides or less," without considering the function of each slide or appreciating the power of the story structure.

The **7-Slide Solution™** is more than a way of presenting. It is a way of thinking. A way that has been proven effective over centuries of use by wise men and women who recognized the power of stories to communicate ideas.

Make it your own way of thinking and you will realize new insights into your business and career, greater acceptance of your ideas, and an ability to really break through the noise of modern business life.

All in 7 slides or less!

Sources

Cognitive Science

Csikszentmihalyi, Mihaly

> *Flow: The Psychology of Optimal Experience.* New York: Harper Perennial, 1991.

Damasio, Antonio R.

> *Descartes' Error: Emotion, Reason, and the Human Brain.* New York: Grosset/Putnam Books, G.P. Putnam's Sons, 1994.

> *The Feeling of What Happens: Body and Emotion in the Making of Consciousness.* New York: Harcourt Brace and Company, 1999.

> *Looking for Spinoza: Joy, Sorrow, and the Feeling Brain.* Orlando: Harcourt, Inc., 2003

Dennett, Daniel C.

> *Consciousness Explained.* Boston: Little, Brown and Company, 1991.

Gardner, Howard

> *The Mind's New Science: A History of the Cognitive Revolution.* New York: Basic Books, 1985.

> *Changing Minds: the Art and Science of Changing Our Own and Other People's Minds.* Boston: Harvard Business School Press, 2004.

Gilovich, Thomas

> *How We Know What Isn't So: the Fallibility of Human Reason in Everyday Life.* New York: The Free Press, 1991.

Gladwell, Malcolm

> *Blink: The Power of Thinking Without Thinking.* New York: Little, Brown and Company, 2005.

Gregory, Richard L.

> *The Oxford Companion to the Mind.* New York: Oxford University Press, 1987.

Hayes, John R.

> *The Complete Problem Solver.* Philadelphia: The Franklin Press, 1981.

Hogarth, Robin M.

Judgement and Choice: the Psychology of Decision. New York: John Wiley and Sons, 1987.

Hunt, Morton

The Universe Within: A New Science Explores the Human Mind. New York: Simon and Schuster, 1982.

Klapp, Orin E.

Overload and Boredom: Essays of the Quality of Life in the Information Society. Westport, CT: Greenwood Press, 1986.

Norman, Donald A.

Learning and Memory. San Francisco: W.H.Freeman and Company, 1982.

Pinker, Steven

How the Mind Works. New York: W.W.Norton & Company, 1997.

Schank, Roger C.

Tell Me a Story: A New Look at Real and Artificial Memory. New York: Charles Scribner's Sons, 1990.

The Connoisseur's Guide to the Mind: How, We think, How We Learn, & What it Means to be Intelligent. New York: Summit Books, 1991.

Smith, Anthony

The Mind. New York: The Viking Press, 1984.

Stories

Cornog, Evan

The Power and the Story: How the Crafted Presidential Narrative Has Determined Political Success from George Washington to George W. Bush. New York: The Penguin Press, 2004.

Frey, James N.

How to Write a Damn Good Novel. New York: St Martin's Press, 1987.

McKee, Robert

Story: Substance, Structure, Style, and Principles of Screenwriting. New York: Regan Books, 1997.

Stein, Sol

> *Stein on Writing.* New York: St Martin's Press, 1995.

Designing Visuals

Krug, Steve

> *Don't Make Me Think: A Common Sense Approach to Web Usability.* Indianapolis: New Riders Publishing, 2000.

Tufte, Edward R.

> *The Visual Display of Quantitative Information.* Cheshire, CT: Graphic Press, 1983.

> *Envisioning Information.* Cheshire, CT: Graphic Press, 1990.

> *Visual Explanations: Images and Quantities, Evidence and Narrative.* Cheshire, CT: Graphic Press, 1997.

> *The Cognitive Style of PowerPoint.* Cheshire, CT: Graphic Press, 2003.

Wurman, Richard Saul

> *Information Anxiety 2.* Indianapolis: Que, 2001.

Other Subjects

Best, Joel

> *Damned Lies and Statistics.* Berkeley: University of California Press, 2001.

De Becker, Gavin

> *The Gift of Fear: Survival Signals that Protect Us from Violence.* Boston: Little, Brown and Company, 1997.

Johnson, Steven

> *Interface Culture: How New Technology Transforms the Way We Create and Communicate.* San Francisco: HarperEdge, 1997

Lewis, Michael

> *Altering Fate: Why the Past Does Not Predict the Future.* The Guilford Press, 1997.

Negroponte, Nicholas

> *Being Digital.* New York: Alfred A. Knopf, 1995.

Paulos, John Allen

> *Innumeracy: Mathematical Illiteracy and Its Consequences.* New York: Vintage Books, 1988.

Werner, J. Severin and Tankard, James W. Jr.

> *Communication Theories: Origins, Methods, and Uses in the Mass Media.* New York: Longman, 1992.

Shenk, David

> *Data Smog: Surviving the Information Glut.* San Francisco: HarperEdge, 1997.

INDEX

The 7-Slide Solution™ Seminar

Since 1990, The Silvermine Consulting Group, LLC has designed and delivered training and development solutions for organizations around the world. As part of that mission, we offer the **7-Slide Solution**™ Seminar so that your organization can increase the effectiveness of its communications, save valuable meeting time, and streamline decision-making.

Any professional who is required to communicate important information – internally or externally – can benefit from this seminar by learning how to:

- Identify the key elements of a compelling business story.
- Design each slide of the presentation as a scene that raises a question, evokes an emotion, answers the question, and bridges to the next slide.
- Use a storyboard to display the story before designing the presentation.
- Exploit the unique role of each slide to engage the audience and create the desire to "see what happens next..."
- Evaluate persuasiveness by measuring audience reaction.

The **7-Slide Solution**™ Seminar has a proven track record of success both in the results participants have been able to achieve and the changes it has made in their lives.

For More Details
Go To:
www.7-SlideSolution.com
Or Call:
203•454•1777

Paul J. Kelly is the founder and principal of the Silvermine Consulting Group, LLC of Westport, CT and has been a management consultant for more than 25 years. Working with Fortune 500 companies such as Pepsi Cola, Pfizer, Shell, Colgate-Palmolive, Pitney Bowes, and many others, he designs and conducts seminars around the world. The author of *Situational Selling: Six Keys to Mastering the Complex Business Sale*, Mr. Kelly is frequently quoted in leading business publications and is a regular speaker at international conferences. He has been developing the practices and techniques of the **7-Slide Solution™** for more than ten years, and has tested and validated them with hundreds of seminar participants from around the world.

265245

Made in the USA